grow THE F*CK up

THE HEALTHY WAY TO IMPROVE YOUR WORK, LIFE BALA

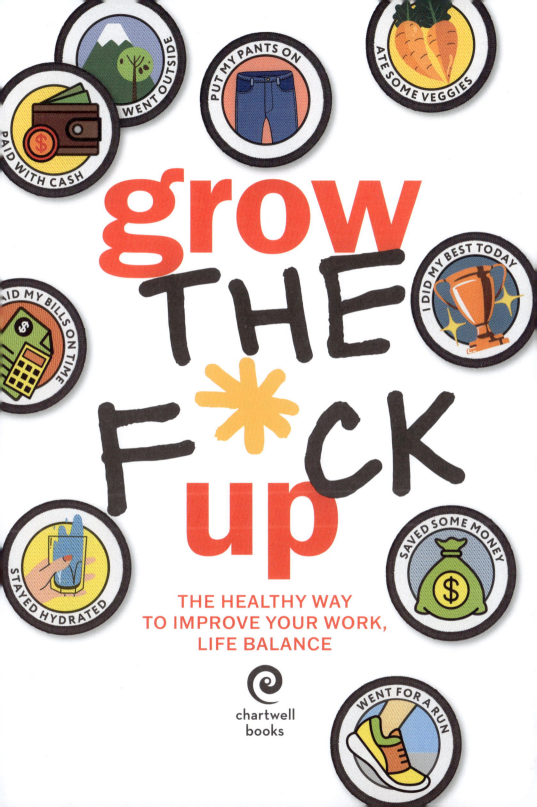

THE ADULT THIS BOOK BELONGS TO:

WELCOME TO ADULTING
(Where Growing Up Doesn't Have to Be a Struggle)..........................6

CHAPTER 1... 14

HOW "ADULT" DO YOU FEEL RIGHT NOW?
AN ADULTING INTAKE SHEET

CHAPTER 2 34

HEALTH, WELLNESS, AND YOU
YOUR GUIDE TO BEING A HEALTHY ADULT

CHAPTER 3 80

FINANCES 101
HOW TO HANDLE YOUR MONEY LIKE AN ADULT

CHAPTER 4 110

I'M WORKING ON IT!
CAREER AND EMPLOYMENT

CHAPTER 5 136

HOME IS WHERE THE ADULT IS
(THAT'S YOU)

CHAPTER 6 158

YOU AND ME
HOW TO HAVE HEALTHY RELATIONSHIPS

YOUR NEXT STEPS (Going Out into the Adult World) 180
APPENDIX (Adulting Tips They Didn't Teach You in School) 184

Welcome to Adulting

(Where Growing Up Doesn't Have to Be a Struggle)

What is "adulting" anyway? As children, it seemed that we spent so much time eagerly waiting to grow up, to be old enough to do whatever we wanted, whenever we wanted. However, no one ever told us that becoming an adult means doing taxes, trying to make friends with other "adults," and learning that just because you *can* order pizza for dinner every night doesn't mean that *you* should. Stepping into adulthood means learning to somehow balance an ever-changing budget, plunging your own toilet, and cleaning out the fridge every so often. But the dirtiest secret of all? No one *knows what they're doing.*

The road to adulthood is not a linear path, especially in our nonstop world. Milestones look different for everyone because everyone has different starting points in life, different goals, and unique challenges and advantages that can make some milestones easy and others feel impossible. We tend to focus on big achievements like getting married, buying a car, getting a promotion at work, and having children.

However, no one tells us that these big moments are created through hundreds of other mini milestones: creating a budget, eating healthy, writing a cover letter, and doing the small tasks that make life, life! While these might not *seem* like major achievements, especially in the age of social media where it looks like everyone is more successful than you, remember that things like going outside, learning basic cooking skills, and making important appointments improve your life in the long term. Don't be fooled by social media; influencers are still struggling to do the dishes, just like the rest of us.

Because adulting doesn't come with a manual, here's the next best thing. *Grow the F*ck Up* is here to help you fake it till you make it. This guided workbook is one part habit tracker, one part advice guide, and one part cheerleader, giving you tips and tricks on a variety of adulting subjects. Sure, your boss won't give you a ribbon for not crying at your desk—but we will! By following along with this book, you can earn such milestone badges as:

Again, while these may seem like simple things, achieving them can lead to *big* changes and make your life easier. Putting the dishes away means you won't have to search for pans and forks while you're trying to cook; this makes it more likely you'll actually cook a healthy meal instead of ordering takeout. Making a phone call means you can schedule that doctor's appointment and take care of your health. Not spending so much time on social media means you'll have more time to be productive at home, get work done, and even develop a new, screenless hobby.

Small steps = big successes. Remember, life's a marathon, not a race.

We know that developing a habit isn't easy, but who doesn't love the feeling of checking something off a to-do list and earning a reward, even if it's a silly badge? By developing a reward system, you are more likely to stick to your habits. By giving you a badge, we (and you) acknowledge that you did a great job and should keep up the hard work. This book will also guide you through the process of achieving your goals and demystifying the process, giving you writing prompts to help you understand why you might struggle with these areas and how you can find a way through—at your own pace. Remember, your journey is your own; we're just here to help.

As anyone who's ever been on their own for even just a little while can attest, there's a lot to adulting. While this book can't possibly cover every aspect, it will cover the biggies. Adulting subjects include:

- Health and wellness
- Financial management
- Employment and career
- Home
- Relationships

Along with an initial "Adulting Intake Sheet," these chapters will review your goals, hopes, dreams, and struggles at the start of your journey. Along with that, you'll see writing prompts, sections for notes, ways to track your goals and achievements, and a "How adult do I feel right now?" scale to track your progress. The good news is you don't have to go through this book in order. Adulting, like everything else in life, has seasons. In some seasons of your life, you will need more help in your "home" area than any other. In other seasons, you will be more focused on the career and health chapters. Remember, everyone's journey in life will be different, so start where you are. Feel free to skip around the book when needed, focusing on the areas you struggle with first and seeing where life takes you.

How to Use This Book

Rome wasn't built in a day and neither are good habits. According to experts, it takes about 66 days for an action to become routine. By creating small habits and building them over time, you can achieve big things. While "getting your life" together may seem like an overwhelming task, start this workbook by filling out the "Adulting Intake Sheet" in Chapter 1 to help you decide what area of your life needs the most focus. Then, in each chapter, you'll take your goals and break them down into smaller actions. Want a new career in a new country? A difficult goal! But if you break it down into small tasks such as polishing your resume, checking for new jobs daily, and learning the process of how to move to a new country, your goal starts to take shape. This is a better way than just quitting your job and hoping for the best or sitting there "wishing" for things to change.

*Grow the F*ck Up* is filled with handy habit-tracking charts to track your progress, create goals, and help you think of rewards (other than badges) to keep you motivated and focused (see page 12 for a sample).

Write your goals, and for every day that you meet them, simply check the box. By checking off tasks, you'll be more likely to continue the behavior. To help keep you on track, though, think about what motivates you to achieve those goals—all the ways making these changes toward your goals will make you feel better—and jot down some thoughts.

To further motivate you, think about how you can reward yourself for achieving your goals. Positive rewards can take many forms, including privileges, activities, recognition, and tangibles like badges. These rewards train your brain to feel good, and after a little while, those good feelings will be their own reward. Come back to these charts as you add more goals. Copy them into notebooks or journals when you need to.

Also look for "Adulting Hacks" with more practical life advice and "Adulting Challenges" to get you over the hurdle of trying something new or difficult. We never said change was easy, but it can still be fun! Think of this workbook as your accountability buddy, acting as your cheerleader to help you achieve your goals. While sections of this book will give you "deadlines," don't give up if you don't meet them on time. Life may give us challenges, but it's up to us to keep going. Applaud all the successes you did have, *clapping* and keep trying.

So let's start adulting!

SAMPLE HEALTHY HABITS TRACKER

Goal	Mon	Tue	Wed
Do 15 minutes of yoga	○	○	○
Add $10 to my savings account	○	○	○
Check in with a friend	○	○	○
Make my bed	○	○	○
	○	○	○
	○	○	○
	○	○	○
	○	○	○
	○	○	○
	○	○	○
	○	○	○
	○	○	○
	○	○	○
	○	○	○

List goals for the week

List rewards for reaching goals

List what keeps you on track for the week

Rewards for the week:

Getting a new book from the library

A walk along the beach

Motivation:

Feel like a better adult

WEEK OF

Thu	Fri	Sat	Sun	
○	○	○	○	
○	○	○	○	
○	○	○	○	
○	○	○	○	
○	○	○	○	
○	○	○	○	
○	○	○	○	
○	○	○	○	
○	○	○	○	
○	○	○	○	
○	○	○	○	
○	○	○	○	
○	○	○	○	
○	○	○	○	

check off days you complete tasks

What to improve for next week:

Up the ante for next week or try again—we're not here to judge!

CHAPTER 1

HOW "ADULT" DO YOU FEEL RIGHT NOW?

An Adulting Intake Sheet

Have you ever been in a situation where you looked around and asked yourself, "Where's the adult?" and came to the horrible realization that it's you, you're the adult? Don't worry, it has happened to just about everyone. One day you're carefree and wild and then suddenly your back hurts when you get up in the morning, and you have to pay for life insurance.

Adulting comes at you fast, especially when life throws you a few curveballs. When you're on your own facing new situations, you may feel as if you missed a chapter in life. "Did I miss that day in class when everyone else learned this?" "Is everyone struggling like I am?" "Why am I having such a difficult time?" In the age of social media, where we get the (false) impression that everyone seems to have it all figured out, believe us when we say that everyone struggles at different areas in their lives at different times based on a variety of factors. You are not alone.

By purchasing this book, you've acknowledged that you need help being an "adult," at least in some areas. So give yourself a round of applause. *clapping* Knowing you need some assistance is the first step to getting on the right track.

So where do you start? We understand that this can be an overwhelming question, especially if your answer is "everywhere and all the things!" Fortunately, we're going to take it one step at a time by understanding where you currently are in your adulting journey. By understanding where you are and where you have been, you can chart your destination.

Let's get started!

> It bears repeating: Adulting is not linear. You know yourself best, and not everything in these pages will apply to you. We all know that every adult is unique, and all our journeys might not line up together. Just take what we've written here and think about things from a different perspective. This is an opportunity to think creatively about your own life, your skill set, and your abilities. You do you.

Pre-Adulthood

To understand how you got to this point in your life, you need to look back on what brought you here. This section will reflect on your childhood, the adults around you as you grew up, and the lessons and challenges you had that made you the person you are today. Once you know where you've been, you can understand how to move forward.

→ When did you first feel like an adult? Was it when you went to college? Started your first job? Had a child? Something else? Write about this time: how old you were, what you were doing, and how it made you feel. If you've *never* felt like an adult, write about the time you were first treated as one.

→ We often learn how to become an adult from the adults who took care of us. Who raised you? Write about who took care of you as a child and what kind of person or "adult" they were.

→ Did you have a mentor growing up? Write about them and what kind of person they were. Why did you look up to them? Do you see their influence in your life today?

→ What was the best lesson(s) that the people who raised you and/or mentor taught you growing up? These can be emotional lessons such as "My parents taught me what a healthy relationship looks like" or practical ones like "My grandfather taught me how to change a tire." Go as deep as you want. How do you use these lessons today?

→ What are some of the lessons or areas the people who raised you failed to touch on during your childhood, and how do they affect you today? It may be that your parents never discussed money in front of you or were bad at financial planning. Maybe you didn't know about any family health problems till much later in life. Write about these gaps in your "adulting" knowledge and how they affect you now.

→ Growing up, what are some of the things that happened that made parts of your adulthood easier? Did you not need to take on student loans or credit card debt early on? Did you have a healthy relationship with your family that makes life easier now? Write about it and how it makes your current life more comfortable.

→ What challenges did you face growing up that have affected your adulthood today? Maybe you grew up with health challenges or grew up in a family with financial issues. Whatever it is, write about it here, including your feelings about it.

→ Think back to when you were a child. What did you think an "adult" was? What did you think adults did? Were you excited to grow up? In what way has adulthood met or not met your expectations?

Adulting Checklist (or, Just Doing Your Best)

While every adult is "different" with different milestones to achieve, there are some basics nearly everyone needs to reach to build a solid base for their adult life. To help understand how much of an "adult" you are, here's a checklist of adulting basics. **Don't be ashamed if you don't check everything off this list right now or cannot cross things off because of your life circumstances.** *This list is meant to reflect on and highlight the areas in your life that you may want to pay more attention to so you can check them off later. So be honest—no one is here to judge you!*

ADULTING INTAKE SHEET	
○ Have a paying job	○ File taxes yearly
○ Can cook at least one meal for yourself	○ Can get yourself to places on time
○ Pay your bills on time	○ Have a healthy relationship (family, romantic, platonic, etc.)
○ Have your important paperwork (birth certificate, social security card, passport, etc.) and keep it in a safe place	○ Have a savings account with some money in it
○ Get an annual health checkup	○ Brush your teeth twice a day

◯ Get dressed and ready daily (change out of different clothing, take a shower, brush hair, etc.)	◯ Have a budget
◯ Have a place to live (that you contribute money towards)	◯ Have a system to organize your important things (from paperwork to home organization, planner, etc.)
◯ Created a will	◯ Have some kind of insurance (medical/dental, homeowner's/ renter's, life, etc.)
◯ Can keep a reasonably clean house (throwing garbage way, vacuuming, cleaning the toilet, not leaving food out, etc.)	◯ Do volunteer work
◯ Set up a debt repayment plan (if needed)	◯ Are able to be there emotionally for a loved one when needed
◯ Are able to accept responsibility for your actions without deflection, denial, or anger	◯ Regulate your emotions
◯ Hydrate regularly	◯ Can find a way to fix something when it is broken
◯ Take care of your body through exercise, healthy eating, and self-care	◯ Are able to be alone for a period of time
◯ Are able to do basic home care	◯ Accept changes to your life with grace and understanding

Your Current Adult Life

→ Take a moment to think about the things you've accomplished so far in your life. What are you most proud of? They can be major milestones, such as being the top in your field or getting married. Or they can be "small" things, like moving out of your hometown or developing a hobby you enjoy. Even just surviving day-to-day is an accomplishment that you should be proud of.

→ Write down the areas in your life where you feel you're thriving, the areas in life that you feel you have the firmest handle on. Do you have a lot of good friends and a healthy relationship? Do you feel like you have a healthy mind, body, and spirit? Write it down and explain why you feel these things are going well in your life. What have you done to make this area in your life thrive? If you don't think you're thriving at all, remember: if you're reading this, you're alive. That's an achievement.

→ What are some areas in your life you're struggling in? List them here and explain why you feel you're struggling. How does it make you feel to be struggling with this? Don't be afraid to be detailed.

Your Ideal Adult Self

→ Now write about your ideal self. The person you want to be when you "grow up." There are hundreds of ways to be an adult, so think about the adult *you* want to be. Go into as much detail as possible, covering every area of your life: where you want to live, the job you want, your friends, your partner, your feelings about yourself. Write as if they've already happened. For example: "I am debt free, I have my own home in a cute, friendly neighborhood, and I have a giant orange cat. I am so happy." Dream big, and don't try to limit your ideas and ambitions.

Adulting Goals

Now that you know about the adult you want to become, let's think about the steps you'll need to take to reach those goals. Even if your dream self seems unreachable now, by setting goals, you can see what areas in your life need the most attention and where to go from there.

You can set these goals in any order. Maybe you want to start by setting your five-year goals and work your way backward. Maybe you want to create simple one-month goals and take it from there. You also don't have to fill this all out now. You can go through the book first to help you discover and shape your goals and go from there. Take it one step at a time to get started on your journey to adulthood!

ONE-MONTH GOALS

Write out three goals you wish to achieve by the end of the month. These don't have to be big goals. Start with small, easy to manage goals, like putting $50 in a savings account or reading a book about a subject you're interested in. You can keep track of them using the habit tracker at the end of each chapter.

→ Goal 1 _____

I will complete this goal by: _____ /_____ /_____

→ Goal 2 _____

I will complete this goal by: _____ /_____ /_____

→ Goal 3 _____

I will complete this goal by: _____ /_____ /_____

The average price of gasoline in 1973 was $0.39 per gallon—the equivalent of $2.72 in 2023 dollars. However, the average price of gas was well over $3 per gallon in 2023, which suggests the dollar doesn't go as far as it did fifty years ago. Not that we needed any proof.

SIX-MONTH GOALS

Now that we have some momentum going, think about where you want to be in six months. Set three goals you wish to achieve during that time. It can be in any area of your life, but try to connect it to the goals you set for one month so you can continue to build on the goal of being your "dream adult self."

→ Goal 1 _____

I will complete this goal by: _____ /_____ /_____

→ Goal 2 _____

I will complete this goal by: _____ /_____ /_____

→ Goal 3 _____

I will complete this goal by: _____ /_____ /_____

ONE-YEAR GOALS

A lot can happen in a year! Think about where you are right now and where you want to be. Set three to five goals you wish to achieve over the course of a year in any area or multiple areas of your life.

→ Goal 1 _____

I will complete this goal by: _____ /_____ /_____

→ Goal 2 _____

I will complete this goal by: _____ /_____ /_____

→ Goal 3 _____

I will complete this goal by: _____ /_____ /_____

→ Goal 4 _____

I will complete this goal by: _____ /_____ /_____

→ Goal 5 _____

I will complete this goal by: _____ /_____ /_____

FIVE-YEAR GOALS

Now that we're thinking about the future, it's time to think about the future adult you. What do you want to achieve to help you become your dream adult self? Set three to five goals you want to achieve in five years.

→ Goal 1 _____

I will complete this goal by: _____ / _____ / _____

→ Goal 2 _____

I will complete this goal by: _____ / _____ / _____

→ Goal 3 _____

I will complete this goal by: _____ / _____ / _____

→ Goal 4 _____

I will complete this goal by: _____ / _____ / _____

→ Goal 5 _____

I will complete this goal by: _____ / _____ / _____

Okay, we've made our first step into being an adult: understanding what we need to do! Now that you know which areas in your life are a little lacking, or the goals you want to achieve, it's time to get started. You can either go through this book in order, or you can flip to the chapter where you need the most help. For example, if you need help with finances, head on over to Chapter 3.

Good luck! You got this!

CHAPTER 2

HEALTH, WELLNESS, AND YOU

Your Guide to Being a Healthy Adult

The most precious thing in our lives is our health. That's because it affects every part of our lives: our finances, our careers, where we live, and our relationships. Everything relies on how healthy we are. Missing a yearly teeth cleaning can lead to costly fillings or dental surgery later. Having multiple sick days can hurt your performance at work. Feeling fragile may make you miss events with friends.

Unfortunately, we often take our health for granted until something goes wrong. You might be feeling great now, but if haven't been treating your body kindly (not getting yearly checkups, not eating the best foods, not getting enough sleep, and avoiding exercise like the plague), you might be inviting health challenges down the road. Or maybe you're dealing with old or even new health issues, and you need to manage your "new normal." If you want to become your dream adult self, you need to take responsibility for your health, both physically and mentally, to help you grow as a person.

But before we get started, let's do a brief wellness check-in:

→ **How healthy do you feel right now?**

1 — 2 — 3 — 4 — 5 — 6 — 7 — 8 — 9 — 10

pretty rough ← → healthiest ever

→ **Explain why you feel this way.**

→ How do you feel about your current wellness situation? What health matters concern you? This could be health ailments you're dealing with or worries about your future health. Don't focus just on physical health, think about your mental health as well.

→ Now go over your health history. How has your health and wellness been throughout your life: surgeries, diagnoses, major changes, etc. Write a little about your family health history as well.

→ What areas about your health do you want to change and improve on? Why are they such a struggle for you?

→ What does a healthier life look like to you?

ADULTING HACK

While takeout is delicious and easy, it's not great for your body or your wallet to have it every night. It's important that you learn how to make some easy recipes, even if you don't have a lot of time, skill, or resources. Make it a mission to go on YouTube or other online sources and watch some simple cooking videos (scrambled eggs, pasta, roasted veggies, etc.) to help you get started.

Physical Health

If you thought puberty wreaked havoc on your body, just you wait. No matter how old you are, it seems like every day something new pops up. Whether you now squint while reading or realize that you can't party as hard as you once did, you'll soon realize that your body shifts and adjusts as it gets older. This isn't always a bad thing; if you take care of your body by giving it the proper nutrition, hydrating, exercising, resting, and listening to it when it tells you it needs you, you are doing everything you can to experience a full life. You know your body and its limitations best, so do what's best for you.

Let's look at ways we can adult our way through physical health. Since this is a book—not a doctor's prescription—we'll be drawing attention to your daily habits, encouraging you to find what's working for you and what you can improve on.

It's always important to check in with your doctor before making any major changes to your diet or exercise regimen.

EATING NUTRITIOUSLY

Whether you live to eat or eat to live, we all have a hunger that must be satisfied. However, we rarely realize what we put into our bodies, or when we do it. How often do you sit in front of your TV with a bag of chips and suddenly they're gone? Or spend all day working and realize at 9:00 p.m. you haven't eaten?

In the exercise on the next couple pages, you're going to write down everything you eat in one day. Don't suddenly eat differently just because you're writing it down. This is simply an exercise in mindful eating. By keeping track of what you eat in a day and how you were feeling when you ate, you can begin to understand your eating habits. After journaling what you ate in a day, you'll reflect on what you noticed and learned.

Remember that your nutritional needs will change over your life, so don't get too hung up on fads and eating trends. Focus on what makes your body feel good. If you notice some foods (even your favorites) don't make you feel the best, it might be time to talk to a professional about dietary changes. You only have one body in this lifetime; take care of it and it'll take care of you.

MINDFUL EATING TRACKER

BREAKFAST

Time

Your Meal

How did you feel before eating?

How did you feel after eating?

LUNCH

Time

Your Meal

How did you feel before eating?

How did you feel after eating?

DINNER

Time

Your Meal

How did you feel before eating?

How did you feel after eating?

SNACKS

Times you had a snack

Your Snacks

Why did you choose these snacks?

How did you feel after eating them?

MINDFUL EATING REFLECTION QUESTIONS

Recording what you eat can be a very enlightening exercise because you have to take notice of what you're eating and how much. Sometimes, our lives get so busy we are often on autopilot during mundane tasks like eating and drinking. But once you sit down and notice what you're eating, you become aware of your body again. This is called mindful eating.

→ What were some food habits you recognized? For example, maybe you realized that you eat most of your snacks late at night or that you have your big meal in the afternoon. Reflect on why you do this.

→ What foods made you feel good either during or after eating? Describe why.

→ What foods made you feel bad either during or after eating? Describe why.

→ Brainstorm how you can reduce those bad feelings. Maybe your stomach hurts after eating a lot of bread or ice cream; you might want to look into the cause. If you feel guilty after eating a lot of junk food, you might want to look for the emotional cause of that.

→ How would you describe your current relationship with food? Was it always this way?

→ What would be your ideal relationship with food?

→ What does hunger feel like to you?

ADULTING CHALLENGE

Continue to track your meals for at least one week, and identify something you'd like to improve in your diet: ditching one soda each day, actually eating that salad mix you bought, remembering to eat dinner each night. Use the habit tracker on page 76 to check your progress and claim your badge on page 79.

→ Do emotions ever impact your eating habits? In what ways?

ADULTING CHALLENGE

Take something you identified in the previous challenge that you'd like to improve in your diet and add that to your habit tracker on page 76. Maybe you'll cook all your dinners this week instead of getting fast food, or you'll take a short walk when the afternoon hangries hit, rather than hitting the vending machine. Or maybe you'll just add a new veggie to your plate. Check your progress and claim your badge on page 79.

→ What is your biggest hurdle when it comes to developing and having a nutritious diet?

→ Brainstorm ways you can overcome this hurdle. For example, if you don't have time to cook, you might subscribe to a healthy meal subscription service, or dedicate one day of the week to meal prep.

HELLO, HYDRATION

Bad news: soda does not count as a hydrating liquid. Nor do energy drinks, juices, or your sugar and creamed–filled coffeeshop concoction. Yes, this is a crushing blow. According to most experts, you should aim to drink 6 to 8 glasses of water a day, which works out to be between 48 and 64 ounces. You may be thinking, "Wow, that's a lot of water! Why do we need so much?" Well, partly because our bodies are made up of mostly water, so it's important to keep hydrated, as water helps the body do what it does best: keep us alive.

Here are some things water does for the body—many of which become more crucial as you get older:

- helps increase saliva
- regulates body temperature
- lubricates your joints, spinal cord, and tissues
- gets rid of waste through perspiration, urination, and defecation (gross, but true!)
- keeps up your strength and endurance while exercising
- prevents constipation
- helps digestion and the absorption of nutrients
- improves circulation
- fights off illnesses
- boosts focus, alertness, and short-term memory
- improves mood
- is great for healthy and glowing skin

Fortunately, you don't have to chug plain water all day. Liquids that count toward your water intake include black coffee and tea, sugar-free flavored water, and sparkling water. However, even with all these choices, it can still be a struggle to achieve your recommended daily water intake. Here are some clever ways to reach your goal:

- Set it as a daily goal and track it (make it one of your goals in your habit tracker on page 76).
- Remember: out of sight out of mind, so keep a reusable water bottle with you at all times.
- Drink one glass of water before each meal. (It also helps get you fuller, faster.)
- Set up an alarm on your phone to alert you when it's time to drink more water.
- Drink one glass of water when waking up and one glass before going to bed.
- Eat it. Foods like watermelon, lettuce, celery, zucchini, cabbage, cantaloupe, and honeydew melon all have a high water content.

ADULTING CHALLENGE

Using the habit tracker on page 76, create a hydration goal for yourself, whether that's drinking the recommended 6 to 8 glasses every day for a week, swapping out one caffeinated beverage for water, or just getting more water into your system each day—whatever that means for you. Check your progress and claim your badge on page 79.

THE IMPORTANCE OF EXERCISE

Whether you were the star athlete in high school or tried faking a doctor's note to get out of gym class, moving your body with exercise is a great way to keep your body and mind happy and healthy, no matter what your age. Thanks to our busy lives, however, it can be difficult to find the time and energy to exercise. As an adult, you may be tempted to write yourself a hall pass to skip working out, but when you make the time for it, exercise can help to improve your life in every way.

Most experts agree that adults should aim for at least 30 minutes of moderate physical activity a day. People who have very physical, demanding jobs can meet these goals easily, while those who work in an office may have to work a little harder. It also depends on your body. So what's your activity level? Check this chart to see where you land.

SEDENTARY

- Take fewer than 5,000 steps a day
- Spend most of your time sitting (having an office job and/or spending most of your free time watching TV, reading, or doing hobbies that involve sitting)
- Only move to do basic activities including cleansing, shopping, cooking, taking care of plants, etc.

LIGHTLY ACTIVE

- Take between 5,000 and 7,500 steps a day
- Have all the traits of sedentary but do light exercise one to three times a week (walking, yoga, swimming, light cardio, and light weight training)
- Have a job that requires you to be on your feet for a good part of the day (teacher, cashier, sales reps, etc.)

ACTIVE

- Take between 7,500 and 10,000 steps a day
- Work out 3 to 5 times a week, spending 30 minutes to an hour doing cardio at the gym, hiking, jogging, strength training, spinning, etc.
- Have a job that requires you to be on your feet doing some physical activity (serving, lifeguard, nurse, doctor, parent of a toddler, etc.)

VERY ACTIVE

- Take more than 12,000 steps a day
- Work out 5 times a week doing heavy fitness activities including cardio or intense weight training
- Have a physically demanding job (steel worker, carpenter, firefighter, personal trainer, etc.)

ADULTING HACK

No matter how busy of an adult you are, there are some simple ways to squeeze in exercise every day. Experiment and see what's best for you!

- Get an accountability buddy to work out with to help stay motivated.
- Combine working out with an activity you're already doing (do squats while washing dishes, lift weights while watching TV, dance while you vacuum, go for a walk while making phone calls, etc.).
- Start with 10 minutes and build to higher goals.
- Make daily activities a little more challenging (walk to the coffeeshop, use a push mower, park at the edge of a parking lot, take the stairs at the mall, whip cream by hand instead of with a mixer, etc.).

WHERE TO START

Starting a fitness routine can be pretty intimidating, especially if you aren't sure where to begin or if it's been a while since your last exercise class. Trying to make time to work out isn't always easy, either, but thanks to the internet, you can follow fitness classes in the comfort of your own home, often for free. Here are some exercise options to get you going, arranged by category. People typically need a combination of all four categories in their weekly fitness routine to create a balanced workout.

ENDURANCE, also known as aerobic or cardio exercising, is great for improving your heart, lungs, and circulatory system. It also boosts your endorphins. Endurance activities include:

> As always, if you're new to exercise, consult your doctor or work with a qualified trainer.

- Walking, jogging, or running
- Cycling or spinning
- Yard work (hand mower, raking, etc.)
- Dancing
- Swimming
- Hiking
- Aerobics
- Jumping rope
- Roller skating/ice skating
- Cross-country skiing
- Team sports like basketball, soccer, tennis, or pickleball

BALANCE TRAINING is doing exercises that help strengthen your core muscles, legs, and back to help maintain your balance. These exercises also help prevent falls and injuries and boost cognitive function. Balance activities include:

- Yoga
- Tai chi

STRENGTH TRAINING is when you add weight to your body or make your body move against resistance. It makes you stronger, and stronger muscles can help protect your joints from injury. Strength activities include:

- Weight lifting/weight training
- Using resistance bands
- Squats
- Push-ups and pull-ups
- Weight machines
- Indoor (or outdoor!) rock climbing
- Pilates

FLEXIBILITY EXERCISES can help increase your range of motion, make your joints less tight, and improve your flexibility in your daily life. They can be done before a workout or first thing in the morning. Flexibility exercises include:

- Stretching, including leg, back, and arm stretches
- Yoga
- Pilates
- Ballet

ADULTING CHALLENGE

Pick any of the exercise suggestions, and try it for a week (or a set number of days for the week), just to get your body moving. You don't have to do it perfectly or for very long. It could be walking the dog to the park instead of around the block, or jumping rope every morning, or trying a few yoga stretches before bed—whatever works for you. Add it to your habit tracker on page 76. When you're done, claim your badge on page 79.

EXERCISE REFLECTION QUESTIONS

→ What do you like to do for exercise? Even if you're not a gym rat, there are still activities you may enjoy doing, from swimming or jumping on a trampoline, to taking a stroll in the garden. How do these exercises make you feel? How often do you do them?

→ What do you not like about exercising? Are there exercises you hate doing? Does the thought of going to the gym make your skin crawl?

→ What would be your ideal relationship with exercise? What steps do you need to take to get there?

→ How do you feel before working out versus how you feel after?

→ Write out some of your exercise goals. What are you hoping to gain from your fitness journey? More energy? A confidence boost? Lowering your risk for heart disease?

I HAVE TO SEE DOCTORS, *HOW* OFTEN?

When was the last time you've been to the doctor's office that *wasn't* an emergency? More often than not, it's been more than a minute since you've gotten your teeth cleaned and had your physical. Despite the importance of good health, it can be difficult to see a professional about it. From trying to find time in our schedule, getting insurance (and finding someone who takes that insurance), and our own feelings around doctors: all of it can make us put this task at the very end of our "to do" list. You may even think, "I feel fine, why should I go to the doctor?" or worse, "I'm worried that something might be wrong with me, so I don't want to go."

Just because you feel fine today, however, doesn't mean there isn't a medical issue lurking underneath. Taking care of medical issues early can help you get your health back sooner, reduce the risk of potential medical bills, and even save your life. And if everything is fine, it's one less thing to worry about.

So how often should we go to the doctor (and how many do we need to see)? It depends. There're many factors to consider, including your age, medical history, risk factors, lifestyle, and how you feel right now. Take a look at the general list on the next page of how often you should see your doctor, and then flip the page for generally recommended screenings and age guidelines for them.

CHECKUP CHECKLIST

○	**DENTIST**	Ideally, you should see a dentist every six months for a cleaning and checkup, though it is recommended to visit a dentist yearly to make sure you are in good oral health. Beyond contributing to tooth decay and gum disease, poor dental hygiene could increase the risk of heart disease.
○	**OPTOMETRIST**	If you use corrective lenses, you should visit the eye doctor every one to two years, to make sure your prescription is correct. If you don't, you should ideally visit the eye doctor every five years to test for eye conditions including glaucoma, cataracts, or macular degeneration, especially as you get older.
○	**PRIMARY CARE PHYSICIAN**	A primary care physician is a doctor you see for general medical issues and checkups, as they do a bit of everything and can refer you to a specialized doctor, if necessary. For example, if they notice you have a dark mole on your shoulder, they may refer you to a dermatologist. Ideally, you should get a yearly physical, but most doctors recommend getting a checkup every one to three years. Your primary care doctor can perform or order most of the preventive screenings listed on the next page (many of which are fully covered by insurance).
○	**SPECIALISTS**	For example, an annual visit to an Ob/Gyn or an as-needed check-in with a specialist, like a gastroenterologist, allergist, or neurologist, if you have a chronic condition.

PREVENTIVE SCREENING LIST

◯	**BLOOD GLUCOSE TEST**	Every five years, starting at age 30, to test for diabetes.
◯	**BLOOD PRESSURE SCREENING**	Every two years to assess your heart's condition.
◯	**BONE DENSITY TEST**	Every three years, starting in your 40s, to test for osteoporosis.
◯	**CHOLESTEROL SCREENING**	Every five years, starting in your 30s, to test for heart disease.
◯	**COLONOSCOPY**	Every five to ten years, starting at age 45, to test for colorectal cancer and precancerous polyps.
◯	**CORONARY SCREENING**	Year after turning 50 to test for heart disease.
◯	**HEARING TEST**	Every ten years to monitor your hearing.
◯	**MAMMOGRAM**	Yearly, starting at age 40, to check for breast cancer, but consider testing earlier if you have a family history of the disease.
◯	**OVARIAN SCREENING**	Every three years, post menopause, to test for ovarian cancer.
◯	**PELVIC EXAM**	Yearly; pap tests every three years (every five years after age 30) to screen for cervical cancer.
◯	**PROSTATE EXAM**	Yearly after the age of 40.

PREVENTIVE SCREENING LIST

○	**SEXUALLY TRANSMITTED INFECTION (STI) TESTING**	Every three to six months if you have multiple sexual partners and yearly if you don't. You can get an STI test at your yearly physical or at a health clinic.
○	**SKIN EXAM**	Yearly for signs of new moles and potential skin cancer.
○	**TESTICULAR EXAM**	Yearly for risk of cancer.

ADULTING CHALLENGE: MAKE YOUR OWN CHECKUP APPOINTMENT

Maybe this is your first time making your own wellness appointment, or maybe you've relocated and need to start over with new doctors. Or maybe you just don't like going to the doctor or dentist. Whatever the reason you've been avoiding it, now's the time. Choose a visit you've been needing to make.

Do a little research on the doctors in your area. If you have insurance, you can look for doctors in your network. Or, work backwards and ask friends for recommendations, then see if the doctors take your insurance.

If you do not have health insurance, you can still get a yearly physical, but you may have to pay out of pocket. Look for offices that treat patients without insurance and ask about potential payment options before booking your appointment.

Call the office and make the appointment. Put the appointment on your calendar and claim your badge on page 79.

CHECKUP REFLECTION QUESTIONS

→ What is your biggest hurdle about seeing a doctor or other health professional? Did you grow up around someone who was sick and you're left with uneasy feelings? Do you worry you can't afford it? Brainstorm ways you can overcome it.

→ Do you have any fears about seeing a doctor or dentist? If so, write them down here.

Mental Wellness

Your physical health is only one factor in your overall health. You may be in perfect physical health, but if you are having a difficult time mentally or emotionally, you won't be feeling very good at all. Society has made great strides in the last few years to embrace mental health, but there is still a stigma about our mental and emotional needs, even though they are directly related to our overall wellbeing. Being an adult means being able to nurture and maintain your mental health. This can manifest in a variety of ways: learning to cope with emotions and stress, knowing when to put yourself in time-out, and knowing when to ask for help when you need it.

In this section, you'll be reviewing how to navigate your mental health. Let's begin with a couple of questions:

→ How are you feeling, mentally and emotionally?

(1)—(2)—(3)—(4)—(5)—(6)—(7)—(8)—(9)—(10)

grrrrrr ←————————————————→ on top of the world

→ Explain why you feel this way.

→ When was the last time you felt content? Not overly happy and not plain blah. Just very content. Write about this feeling and what you were doing at the time.

→ Do you have any mental health challenges right now or have you had them at some point in your life? How do/did you manage them?

→ When was the last time you did something kind for yourself? What was it?

_____

_____

_____

_____

_____

_____

_____

HOW ARE YOU FEELING TODAY?

Have you ever been to a grocery store and heard a baby crying and think, "I wish I could do that"? No? Just us? Okay... Seriously, when we are young we feel everything for the first time, which makes every emotion so intense. As we get older, however, we learn to regulate and manage our emotions in healthy ways. Well, most of us do. To understand our mental health, it's important to get in touch with our feelings. How often do you check in with yourself? Do you notice that you feel down consistently or are often angry? By paying attention to your moods, you can start gauging your mental health and figure out where to go from here.

MOOD TRACKING

In the following exercise, track your mood for the next few days. Don't try to tone it down—this isn't a graded test. This is to help you reflect on your emotions and feel your feelings.

MOOD TRACKER

Date:

How I feel today:

Three things that happened today:

1.

2.

3.

Three things I'm grateful for:

1.

2.

3.

Hopes for tomorrow:

Date:

How I feel today:

Three things that happened today:

1.

2.

3.

Three things I'm grateful for:

1.

2.

3.

Hopes for tomorrow:

Date:

How I feel today:

Three things that happened today:

1.

2.

3.

Three things I'm grateful for:

1.

2.

3.

Hopes for tomorrow:

→ How did you feel after tracking your moods? What are some big things you noticed?

→ Based on what you found in your tracking, what can you do to improve your mood for the future?

ADULTING CHALLENGE

Using your habit tracker on page 76, track your mood for seven days straight. Once you complete your challenge, claim your badge on page 79.

PRACTICE SELF-CARE

Our definition of self-care has gotten a little distorted over the years thanks to big corporations using the word to sell us stuff. Self-care is anything you do to take care of yourself that helps you stay physically, mentally, and emotionally well. While sometimes this does mean taking a hot bubble bath and eating chocolate cake because you had a hard week, it doesn't mean complete self-indulgence. You can't spend your rent money on shoes in the name of self-care; it'll just create stress later.

Sometimes self-care is boring things such as doing laundry so your future self will have clean clothes to wear, going to bed earlier so you wake up feeling rested, and paying your bills on time so your future self has heat, hot water, and electricity. While it may be hard to take the time out to practice self-care because you're worried it is selfish, imagine your future self: Don't you want to take care of that person?

ADULTING CHALLENGE

Pick one self-care activity (from the next page or an idea of your own) to do every day for a week. It can be the same one daily or you can switch it up. Keep track of it in your habit tracker on page 76. When you've finished, claim your badge on page 79.

ADULTING HACK: INDULGE IN SELF-CARE

Self-care doesn't necessarily mean a spa weekend at a winery (though it certainly could—you work hard for your adult income!). Here is a list of practical, low-cost self-care activities, many of which you can do anywhere.

- Write down your thoughts and feelings in a journal to understand them better.
- Talk to a friend or loved one.
- Eat a meal. Ideally this would be a full, nutritious meal, but do what you can at the moment, even if that's just a handful of cereal.
- Take a hot bubble bath or shower.
- Spend at least ten minutes in the sun.
- Close your eyes and breathe deeply.
- Do the task you've been avoiding for months that has been stressing you out. Trust us, you'll feel better.
- Listen to your favorite music.
- Change into clean clothes that make you feel good.
- Scream into a pillow.
- Exercise.
- Go for a walk in nature (the beach, a park, a forest).
- Pursue a hobby you love.
- Get enough sleep/take a nap.
- Take your medication.
- Practice gratitude.
- Have a good cry.
- Clean one part of your home.
- Talk to a therapist.

Healthy Goals

→ Now that we have a better understanding of how to be a healthy adult, it's time for you to create some goals to get healthy. Write down a list of some of your big health goals.

→ Next, take one of those goals and break it down into smaller actions that can help you achieve it. For example, if your goal is to run a 5K, some of your actionable tasks may be to run every day, drink your recommended amount of water, and get enough sleep so you have all the energy you need to complete your race. Choose at least three smaller goals and write them here.

→ What is your motivation for achieving this health goal from the previous page? Why do you want to? What does it mean for your maturity and growth?

→ Imagine, for a moment, that you have reached that goal. Picture how good it feels. What will you reward yourself with when it's over? A (financially responsible) shopping spree, a book you've been longing for, a vacation? Write it here as a promise to yourself. Also come up with smaller rewards for the smaller tasks you created on page 73 to help you stay on task, motivated, and interested. For example, if you make a healthy dinner every night this week, you'll treat yourself to an episode of your favorite new TV show.

Your major reward:

Mini rewards:

HEALTHY HABITS TRACKER

Goal	Mon	Tue	Wed
	○	○	○
	○	○	○
	○	○	○
	○	○	○
	○	○	○
	○	○	○
	○	○	○
	○	○	○
	○	○	○
	○	○	○
	○	○	○
	○	○	○
	○	○	○
	○	○	○

Rewards for the week:

Motivation:

WEEK OF

Thu	Fri	Sat	Sun	
○	○	○	○	
○	○	○	○	
○	○	○	○	
○	○	○	○	
○	○	○	○	
○	○	○	○	
○	○	○	○	
○	○	○	○	
○	○	○	○	
○	○	○	○	
○	○	○	○	
○	○	○	○	
○	○	○	○	
○	○	○	○	

What to improve for next week:

You are on your way to being your healthiest adult self. However, you don't have to do this alone. Use the habit tracker on the previous page to keep track of your goals and turn mindful actions into healthy adulting habits. And don't forget to reward yourself and claim your badges on the next page.

→ **How adult do you feel right now?**

①—②—③—④—⑤—⑥—⑦—⑧—⑨—⑩

still getting the hang of it ⟵————————⟶ best grown-up around

→ **Final thoughts:**

Claim Your Badges!

CHAPTER 3

FINANCES 101

How to Handle Your Money Like an Adult

They say that the love of money is the root of all evil, but it's a necessary evil as we all need money to live and enjoy life, whether we like it or not. However, while money is an important factor, the way we treat it can vary. Some people spend all their lives on the quest for the all-mighty dollar and never spend a cent, while others spend money like it's going out of style and never have anything for the future. One of the joys of adulthood is making your own money to spend how you please, but being an adult means learning to be responsible with your money so you can invest in your future.

Whether you need help sticking to a budget or thinking about how to use your money to build a stable future, we'll provide the basics to help you control your finances, instead of the other way around.

Before we get started, let's do a brief financial check-in:

→ How wealthy do you feel right now?

(1)—(2)—(3)—(4)—(5)—(6)—(7)—(8)—(9)—(10)

empty piggy bank ← ——————————————→ I'm making bank

→ Explain why you feel this way.

_____

_____

_____

_____

_____

_____

_____

_____

_____

_____

_____

→ What is your current financial situation? How did it get that way?

→ What was the last nonessential thing you purchased? Why did you buy it, and how did you feel after purchasing it?

→ What was your financial situation like growing up? How did the people who raised you handle money? How does that affect you today?

→ What was the biggest financial lesson you learned from the people who raised you?

→ Write about the best financial decision you ever made, how you came to make that decision, why you think it was a good one, and what benefits you've received from it.

→ Write about the worst financial decision you ever made, what made you make that decision, and its consequences. If you could go back in time, what would you do differently?

Adulting on a Budget

Ever since you first started making money, you've probably been told over and over again to budget, budget, budget, but what does that even mean? You likely already understand the basics of budgeting: making sure you have enough money to pay your bills and trying not to let your bank balance get to zero. However, no one tells us how hard budgeting can be when purchases can be made with the swipe of a card or the click of a mouse. Or how your savings can easily be wiped out after a single emergency like a trip to the ER or the refrigerator breaking. Nor do they tell you how often these things can happen. While budgeting is key to financial success, it's important to be flexible with budgeting to allow for potential emergencies, luxuries, and grace.

THE LANGUAGE OF MONEY

Finances can be a pretty intimidating subject, partly because it has to deal with a lot of people's biggest enemy, math, but also because there're so many financial terms that can be difficult to understand, which can leave us discouraged. Financial literacy is something that every single person should become familiar with, as it can prevent you from making financial mistakes while empowering you to put your financial future in your own hands. Here are some financial and budgeting terms you might come across:

COMPOUND INTEREST The interest you earn on a loan or deposit. It is calculated based on the principal (what you initially put in) plus the accumulated interest over time.

DIVIDEND Income earned from owning stocks and shares.

FICO SCORE A person's credit score that has been calculated with software from the Fair Isaac Corporation (FICO). The score is used by banks and other financial institutions to measure a person's creditworthiness; it is calculated based on your credit history, how much you owe in debt, and how regularly you pay your credit debt. A high score means you're more likely to get approved for a loan or new credit card. A low score (below 650) means you may have a harder time getting a loan.

FIXED EXPENSES Monthly expenses that cost the same every month, like your rent or car payment.

NET INCOME Also known as "take home pay," this is the amount of money you make after taxes, 401(k), social security, medical benefits, etc. are taken out. If you're looking at a new job and want to understand what your net income will be, use your gross pay and take out 20 to 30 percent for taxes, 6 percent for social security, and then 1 to 10 percent for retirement (depending on how much you choose to allocate)—there's your approximate net income. *sobs*

NET WORTH Yes, you have a dollar sign on you. Your net worth is calculated by combining your net income plus assets while subtracting your debts and liabilities.

PRE-TAX The money subtracted from your gross pay before taxes are withheld from your paycheck; this includes things like medical benefits and 401(k) contributions. Because it's pre-tax, it lowers the amount you have to pay in income taxes; for example, if your gross pay is $1000, and you have $200 in pre-tax deductions, you'll only have to pay income tax on the remaining $800.

POST-TAX The money left in your paycheck after taxes are taken out. Make it a habit to review your paystub periodically to ensure everything is being allocated as it should; you don't want to wait until tax season to discover that your employer hasn't been taking out enough in federal taxes.

SINKING FUND A set amount of money that you save every month from your income to use for a larger purchase later. For example, if you wanted to save to buy a car, you may take out $200 from your monthly paycheck and put it in a fund just for that.

VARIABLE EXPENSES Expenses that change regularly depending on a variety of factors that make it hard to predict monthly spending. These include things like your gas, grocery, or clothing bill.

Creating a Budget

It doesn't take a financial wizard to know that the cost of living has gone up. To keep your head above water in this expensive world, it's important to know where your money is going and how you can manage it productively to save for your future. So, before we create a budget, let's look at your current spending, earnings, and savings. Pull up your bank and credit statements from last month: all the income you made, everything you purchased, and whatever you put into savings. Every cent counts. Record it all on the next couple pages. If you are married, put your expenses and resources together. If you have children, you can combine their items, like clothing and medical expenses, with yours, or track them separately.

ADULTING HACK: CREATE A RAINY-DAY FUND

Remember, while you may be budgeting to save for a fancy trip or a down payment on a home, it's important to have an emergency fund that you are putting money into for a rainy day—whether that rainy day is losing your job, having an expensive medical bill, or getting a bill for something you weren't expecting. When opening a savings account, start by saving enough money for one month of fixed expenses, then work up to two months and so on until you have at least six months of fixed expenses saved. Don't forget to replenish it, if and when you use it.

EXPENSE TRACKER

INCOME	AMOUNT
Income 1	
Income 2	
Income 3	
Total	

HOUSING	AMOUNT
Mortgage/rent	
Phone	
Electricity	
Gas/oil	
Water/sewer	
Waste removal	
Internet/cable	
Maintenance/repairs	
Supplies	
Other	
Subtotal	

ENTERTAINMENT	AMOUNT
Streaming services/movie rentals	
Music downloads/other purchases	
Movies	
Concerts	
Sporting events	
Theater	
Other event admission	
Other	
Subtotal	

INSURANCE	AMOUNT
Home	
Medical/dental/vision	
Life	
Other	
Subtotal	

TRANSPORTATION	AMOUNT
Vehicle payment	
Bus/taxi/rideshare fare	
Licensing/inspection fee	
Fuel	
Maintenance	
Car wash	
Other	
Subtotal	

CHILD(REN)	AMOUNT
Childcare	
Medical/dental	
Toys/games	
Activities	
Clothing/gear	
Allowance	
Other	
Subtotal	

FOOD	AMOUNT
Groceries	
Dining out	
Coffee/drinks	
Other	
Subtotal	

(continued)

PERSONAL CARE	AMOUNT
Medical/dental	
Hair/nails/massages	
Clothing	
Dry cleaning	
Gym membership/classes	
Organization dues/fees	
Other	
Subtotal	

LOANS	AMOUNT
Personal	
Student	
Credit card	
Credit card	
Credit card	
Credit card	
Other	
Subtotal	

SAVINGS OR INVESTMENTS	AMOUNT
Retirement account	
Investment account	
Savings account	
Other	
Subtotal	

LEGAL	AMOUNT
Attorney	
Alimony	
Other	
Subtotal	

PETS	AMOUNT
Food	
Vet	
Insurance	
Toys	
Grooming	
Boarding/daycare	
Other	
Subtotal	

TAXES	AMOUNT
Federal	
State	
Local	
Other	
Subtotal	

GIFTS AND DONATIONS	AMOUNT
Charity	
Gift	
Donation	
Other	
Subtotal	

TOTAL INCOME	
TOTAL EXPENSES	
DIFFERENCE (income minus expenses)	

→ Notice anything interesting? Where did most of your money go to in your budget? Was it a fixed expense or a variable expense? If it was variable, brainstorm ways you might be able to lower it.

→ What are things in your life that bring you joy? Write them down and how much they cost. Are they worth the cost? Why or why not?

→ Look at your expenses. What are some needless ones you wouldn't miss? Write them here along with how much money you'll save *right now*.

→ What is the biggest change you can realistically make that could improve your financial situation? Are there any smaller changes you could implement?

ADULTING CHALLENGE

Make that "biggest change" and implement it for one week, just to see how realistic that change is for your life. Sometimes, when we cut something (like a streaming service) we barely miss it, but other times that change is all we can think about (like our morning latte). Try cutting something for a week, add it to your habit tracker on page 106, and see where you're at. Once completed, claim your badge on page 109.

BUDGETING TIPS

Now that you know where you've been spending and saving, let's go over some budgeting basics. By now you know you *need* to budget, but where do you even begin? Here are some budgeting tips to get you started in the right direction.

60/20/20 RULE This is a simple way to start budgeting where you take the total of your monthly income and separate it three ways:

- 60 percent of your income goes towards your needs: rent, debt, insurance, groceries, etc.
- 20 percent of your income goes to your wants or "fun money": clothing, concerts, activities, etc.
- 20 percent of your income goes into your savings account

The purpose of this rule is to ensure you don't blow your money and forget about your bills. It also allows you to have some fun money to do with what you please so budgeting doesn't feel like a burden. Remember, it's all about balance.

PAY YOURSELF FIRST If you have a hard time saving money, treat it like a bill. Put aside a certain amount of money each month, and use it to "pay yourself" by putting it into your savings account. Before you spend money on something fun and impulsive, make sure you're paid first.

TRACK EVERY DOLLAR Tracking your money is a great way to help you budget, but remember to track every dollar. Yes, even that $5 latte. Little purchases can lead to major money by the end of the month. Tracking also makes you more mindful about your spending. You're less likely to impulse buy that large houseplant if you know you're going to write it down on your budget sheet.

HAVE BIG AND SMALL GOALS The question isn't how to budget, but what you want to budget for: Paying off debt? Buying a house? Planning a vacation? It's important to have goals when budgeting so you have something to work toward. However, make sure you have small goals as well, like paying off small loans or creating a savings account, to keep you accountable and motivated. Remember that budgets can vary from month to month, so these small goals can also be flexible, like for back-to-school shopping, holiday or birthday gift funds, annual car inspection, annual vet visit, etc.

ADULTING CHALLENGE

Now that you understand budgeting, create your budget using the template on the next page and stick to it for an entire month. (There's a second one if you need it, or if you have a partner you'd like to complete it.) When you succeed, claim your badge on page 109.

MONTHLY BUDGET

MONTHLY INCOME

SOURCE	AMOUNT
Total	

MONTHLY EXPENSES

SOURCE	AMOUNT
Total	

DAILY EXPENSES	MONTHLY SAVINGS

MONTHLY INCOME	
SOURCE	AMOUNT
Total	

MONTHLY EXPENSES	
SOURCE	AMOUNT
Total	

DAILY EXPENSES	MONTHLY SAVINGS

Investing: A Solid Marker of Adulting

Okay, so you're making some money, but what are you going to do with it? You work for money, but your money should be working for you. Financial investments are assets or items one purchases with the goal of generating income or appreciation over time. This can be physical, tangible things like buying a house, or they can be financial products like stocks, bonds, and cryptocurrency that while you can't hold them in your hands, you do own and they can turn a profit for you.

Investing can be intimidating, especially as a lot of it can be risky since earning a profit from an investment is not guaranteed. Making even small investments, however, can help you build wealth and achieve financial goals over time. Let's look into a few investing ideas to consider to help build your portfolio. If any of it seems overwhelming, know that there are financial planners and accountants who can help you out. (Hint: Ask around—no doubt at least one of your friends can recommend someone.)

ADULTING HACK: THE 411 ON FINANCIAL PLANNERS

Once you get the name of an accountant, advisor, or broker, call to set up a meeting. These initial meets are usually free, as they want your business and often earn commission on the plans you buy or the investments you make with them; they may also ask for referrals to your friends and family. It's okay to ask about fees before you meet, and do be prepared to hand over all your sensitive financial information. In return, they'll be able to recommend next steps to improve your financial wellness.

401(k) PLAN A 401(k) is a retirement saving plan that is typically offered by American employers where employees agree to have a percentage of their paycheck paid directly into an investment account. The more you pay in, the more you'll receive at retirement. If you are self-employed, you can still do a 401(k) plan for yourself. This is a great starter investment, as these are taken directly out of your paycheck, and some employers match your contributions; many also have set portfolios that approximate your retirement date, so you don't even have to pick your investments, if that feels overwhelming to you.

INDIVIDUAL RETIREMENT ACCOUNT (IRA) This is a type of retirement saving account where you contribute pre-tax or after-tax money. This money grows on a tax-free basis, giving you more money in the long term. For a traditional IRA (pre-tax), taxes are taken out when you withdraw funds at retirement; for a Roth IRA (after-tax), no taxes are taken out at retirement.

MUTUAL FUNDS A mutual fund lets you pool your money with other investors to buy stock, bonds, and other investments. Mutual funds are run by professional money managers who decide what to buy. This allows you to dip your toe in the investing pool without having to make a lot of decisions, and you share the risk with others, making it less scary.

BONDS A bond is a loan to a government or corporation. Individuals buy a bond for a certain amount with a fixed interest rate, and the government or company agrees to pay back the loan by a certain date. During the period when you hold the bond, your money earns interest at the fixed interest rate. Think of it as an IOU with interest, perfect for a starting investment because it's just a loan.

HIGH YIELD SAVINGS ACCOUNT This is a savings account that has a higher interest on deposits than a regular savings account. This is great for those who are just starting a savings account and want to make a little more money doing it. You won't get rich off it, but your money works harder for you while it sits in your account.

INDIVIDUAL STOCKS Purchasing stocks is the most common form of investing, but it can be a little intimidating, especially as you watch the rise and fall of the stock market. Stocks are how the ownership of major companies are divided up. When you buy stock, you are buying a small share in a company. When a company does well, you do well. If the company does poorly, your shares are worth less. Individual stocks are great for beginners as you are investing in just one company. However, it is riskier because if the company goes belly-up, you'll use money.

ADULTING CHALLENGE

Make an investment today, even if it's a small one like starting a savings account or a figurative investment like researching financial planners. Add it to your habit tracker on page 106. Once you complete your challenge, claim your badge on page 109.

INVESTING REFLECTION QUESTIONS

→ How long have you been investing? If you haven't, why haven't you?

→ What is the hardest thing about investing money? Brainstorm some ways to overcome this hurdle.

Debt & You

While it may be embarrassing to find yourself in debt, it's actually very common. Many people have some kind of debt, including credit card debt, student loan debt, and medical debt, among other kinds of debt. In fact, having a little debt is good because it helps you build credit, which is essential to adult life. However, being overwhelmed by debt you cannot repay on time, or collecting so much interest that you feel you can never pay it off, can affect your financial life as well as your mental health and your future.

Debt is never fun, but here are some ways to aggressively pay it off so you can get back to using that money to build a life.

PAY OFF THE DEBT WITH THE HIGHEST INTEREST RATE It's important to take care of the debt with the highest interest rate first because that is the debt that will increase over time the quickest, leaving you with a much higher bill in the long run. Put all your resources toward that debt, while paying at least the minimum on the others, if that's what you can afford.

PAY MORE THAN THE MINIMUM Most debt will have a minimum monthly payment. You may think, "Oh, I only have to pay $75, that's not bad," but as the interest continues to grow, the minimum won't be enough to pay off your debt. Pay at least double the minimum to get rid of the debt faster.

GET HELP If you're overwhelmed with the amount of debt you have, it might be time to get professional help. Hire an accountant or credit counselor to help you sort through your finances and come up with solutions like consolidating your debts (so you're left with one payment each month).

DEBT REFLECTION QUESTIONS

→ Go through all your accounts, from credit cards to loans (minus a mortgage) and list their balances. How much debt do you have right now?

→ Brainstorm three ways you can pay off some (or even all) of your debt within a year.

Financial Goals

→ Now that we have a better understanding of how to be a financially responsible adult, it's time for you to create some goals to get that money (and save it). Write down a list of your big financial goals.

→ Take one goal and break it down into smaller actions that can help you achieve it. For example, if your goal is to have $5,000 in savings, some of your actionable tasks may be to start a budget, track your spending, and look for extra income. Choose at least three smaller actions and write them here.

→ What is your motivation for achieving this goal? Why do you want to? What does it mean for your maturity and growth?

→ Imagine, for a moment, that you have reached that goal. Picture how good it feels. Write about it as a promise to yourself. Also come up with smaller rewards for the smaller tasks you've created. For example, if you make yourself stick to your budget this week, you'll treat yourself to a day at the beach.

Your major reward:

Mini rewards:

HEALTHY HABITS TRACKER

Goal	Mon	Tue	Wed
	○	○	○
	○	○	○
	○	○	○
	○	○	○
	○	○	○
	○	○	○
	○	○	○
	○	○	○
	○	○	○
	○	○	○
	○	○	○
	○	○	○
	○	○	○
	○	○	○

Rewards for the week:

Motivation:

WEEK OF

Thu	Fri	Sat	Sun	
O	O	O	O	
O	O	O	O	
O	O	O	O	
O	O	O	O	
O	O	O	O	
O	O	O	O	
O	O	O	O	
O	O	O	O	
O	O	O	O	
O	O	O	O	
O	O	O	O	
O	O	O	O	
O	O	O	O	
O	O	O	O	

What to improve for next week:

You are on your way to being your most financially savvy adult self. However, you don't have to do this alone. Use the habit tracker on the previous page to keep track of your goals and turn mindful actions into healthy adulting habits. And don't forget to reward yourself and claim your badges on the next page.

→ How adult do you feel right now?

1 — 2 — 3 — 4 — 5 — 6 — 7 — 8 — 9 — 10

still getting the hang of it ← ───────→ best grown-up around

→ Final thoughts:

CHAPTER 4

I'M WORKING ON IT!

Career and Employment

While Chapter 3 was all about money, this chapter is all about making that money. And while we may all dream of winning the lottery or having a rich distant relative pass and leave us everything so we no longer have to do the grind, most of us will need to work for a living. However, working doesn't have to be a miserable experience. Whether you're trying to find your life's passion, or you just want something you don't despise that lets you pay the bills, this chapter is all about how to find and keep an adult job without hating your life.

Before we get started, let's do a brief career check-in:

→ How employed do you feel right now?

(1)—(2)—(3)—(4)—(5)—(6)—(7)—(8)—(9)—(10)

checking the want ads ←——————————————→ I'm the boss

→ Explain why you feel this way.

→ Write a little about your current job: your job title, the types of tasks you perform, the place you work for, etc. If you are between jobs (or if this is your first time looking for work) write about your last job (or the last time you got paid to do work, whatever that may be).

→ What was your dream job as a child? While we can't all be astronauts or rock stars, understanding the career(s) you wanted as a child can help you understand what sort of career you may want now. For example, did you want to be a firefighter when you were a kid because you like the idea of helping people while also doing something brave?

→ What is your current dream job? It could be something in your current field, like becoming a manager or leveling up to being the boss, or it could be a job in a completely different field. Write about this dream career and why you want it. If you don't have a dream job, write about things you like to do and want to be paid for doing.

→ Think of three career milestones you have already achieved so far. These can be big like getting a promotion, winning a major award, or getting an advanced degree. Or they can be simple like getting a job, developing bonds with coworkers, or learning how to create spreadsheets.

→ Write about three milestones you wish to achieve in your career. This can be at your current job or your dream job. For example, if you're a writer, your major milestone might be publishing a book. If you're a plumber, your major milestone might be starting your own business.

Getting the Job

While we're willing to do the work, finding the right job (or any job) is a career in and of itself. Applying for jobs takes a ton of time, energy, and patience as we search the internet for potential jobs, filling out countless questionnaires and tests, just hoping that someone will get back to us. Whether this is your first job or your hundredth, we're going to walk you through the steps of getting the job you want.

STEP 1: THE RESUME

A resume is a document that acts as a mini-biography of your working life: your educational background, your skills, accomplishments, and previous employment. While a resume can be used for a variety of purposes (getting into college, scholarships, loans, etc.), it is mainly used for getting a job. Resumes can feel pretty intimidating, especially if you're starting from scratch. So, we have some handy tips to make the process go a lot smoother.

TAILOR YOUR RESUME TO THE JOB YOU'RE APPLYING FOR It's important to make your resume a living document, which means you have a basic template that you can add to and edit when needed, especially if you're applying to a variety of jobs. The resume you send when you're looking for a job at a restaurant will not be the same resume you use when applying to teaching jobs, even if they both use similar skills. So make sure you edit your resume for each job you apply to.

ADD KEYWORDS Today, many resumes are scanned using computer software before they even reach a human. Your resume can easily be rejected by a robot, simply because it didn't see any of the qualities it's meant to look for. When writing your resume, look at the qualifications and keywords on the job notice and include them on your resume. For example, if the job requires "Excel skills" and "five years' experience in computer programming," make sure those words are in your resume somewhere (and that you actually have those skills, or you will have problems later).

KEEP IT SHORT AND SIMPLE While this has been hotly debated over the years, most employers and career professionals agree that a resume should be a single page long and contain only your contact information, your educational background, skills, and your last three jobs that relate to the job you're applying for. You don't need to talk about your days at the pizza place in high school if you're applying for a banking job in your 30s.

USE ACTION WORDS When writing about the work you did at previous jobs, don't talk about the basic tasks such as answering phones or taking notes. Showcase the valuable skills and tasks you handled using action words that show how you would be an asset at this new job. Look at the phrases in the box on the next page for examples.

TO SAY	USE
You led a project	coordinated, directed, delegated, orchestrated, organized, planned, programmed
You brought a project to life	developed, established, implemented, launched, initiated, created
Your work helped your company	accelerated, achieved, advanced, capitalized, consolidated, expanded, maximized, reduced, saved, improved
You changed something in your old job	clarified, converted, digitized, merged, modernized, overhauled, redesigned, revamped, streamlined, transformed, updated
You've managed a team	directed, facilitated, guided, hired, mentored, motivated, recruited, shaped, supervised, trained, unified
You brought new things to your company	acquired, negotiated, pitched, partnered, secured, signed
You performed customer support tasks	advised, advocated, consulted, fielded, informed, resolved
You conducted research	analyzed, compiled, discovered, evaluated, explored, identified, investigated, protected, measured, forecasted, reported, surveyed, tracked
You achieved something	completed, earned, exceeded, won, outperformed, showcased, succeeded

BUILDING A RESUME

In this section, we'll be putting together a resume that you can use to get your dream job (or any job). While you can certainly tailor this resume to a job you're applying for, you can also use this resume template as a "master resume," holding all of your skills, work experience, and education in one place; that way you can pick and choose what to add in your other resumes down the line. This is great for creating your first resume or if you aren't looking for a job at the moment but want a resume for "just in case"—especially if you are up for a promotion at work or need to look for a job in a hurry.

ADULTING CHALLENGE

Review the resume on the following page, then fill in the blanks on page 119. Finalize it on your computer and save it with your full name and the word "resume." If you're sending multiple resumes that have been tailored to various companies, it's a good idea to include the company's name, as well, to help you keep track; for example, "John Doe_resume_Company Name." When you complete this challenge, claim your badge on page 135.

YOUR NAME

Email address
Phone number
Website/LinkedIn (not social media channels)

Work Experience

Job Title
Company name • How long you worked there
-
- .... Write three things you did at
- that job using your action words. List up to 3 jobs.

Job Title
Company name • How long you worked there
-
-
-

Education

Degree or certification title ----------- Write about your education and the degree(s) you have. If you did not go to college, write about any certificates or training you've had. You do not need to put that you graduated from high school.

School or organization
Year graduated or earned
-
-
- .... Write any important information about your education like summa cum laude, awards won, or what kind of training you had.

Skills

-
-
-
- .... Write 5 to 7 relevant skills.
-
-
-

_____

_____

_____

_____

Work Experience

_____

- _____
- _____
- _____

_____

- _____
- _____
- _____

Education

_____

_____

_____

- _____
- _____
- _____

Skills

- _____
- _____
- _____
- _____
- _____
- _____
- _____

STEP 2: THE COVER LETTER

For some jobs, you only need a resume to get an interview. For many jobs, however, the resume's main task is to get your potential employer to read your cover letter. A cover letter is a document that acts as an introduction between you and your potential employer. It is meant to review any skills and experience related to the job and explain things that are, and are not, in your resume. While a cover letter sounds daunting, it can actually help your employer get to know more about you and see a bit of your personality. If they like what they read, they will invite you to do an interview.

A cover letter also gives you a chance to talk about why you may be a good fit for the position as well as point out things in your resume. If you had a gap in your resume because you were doing volunteer work, write about that. If you basically built your former company from the ground up, write about that. This is also a way to highlight skills that didn't necessarily come from your previous job. For example, if a job is looking for people with leadership skills, you can write about how you are the captain of your local pickleball team and how those skills can factor into this position.

Like a resume, a cover letter should only be about a page long. Look to the next page to see how a cover letter should be organized.

ADULTING HACK: DRESS FOR THE JOB YOU WANT

Before your interview, do some research into the company's dress culture. Is this a bank or a daycare? Rule of thumb is that you should dress a little more conservatively during an interview (blazer, dress pants, nice top, sensible shoes, no dramatic makeup or perfume/cologne). However, if your industry is a little more formal, dress up. If you are applying for a job at a university, wear the school colors. First impressions matter, so make sure even your clothing stands out.

PARAGRAPH 1 Introduce Yourself

The introduction should only be a couple sentences long addressing who you are, the position you're applying for, and why you would like to work at this company or in this position. This is a chance to showcase that you've done your research (and butter them up a little).

PARAGRAPH 2 A Longer Introduction

This is where you share a bit more about yourself and your work history. This doesn't have to be your whole life story—"I was born on a snowy January morning"—but should talk about what brought you to this point in your life. You can lead with your education: "I graduated from Adult University in 2019 with a B.S. in Chemistry. During my study I focused on..." Or you can talk about your career highlights: "While my mother said I was born with the gift of gab, my first real communication job was at Adult Industries where I..." Be professional but make it a little personal. This section should be three to five sentences long.

PARAGRAPH 3 Add a Hero Story

A hero story is a short anecdote about a key part of yourself you want to highlight to your hirer. This can be used to draw attention to a certain skill you have, a special thing you have done, and prove why you should be interviewed and hired. (There's a formula for a great hero story on the next page.)

PARAGRAPH 4 Ending and Thank You

End the letter by telling them how excited you are to meet with them and what you would bring to the table if they hire you. This is a great time to mention your contact info again, when you are available for an interview, and even a potential start date. Remember to thank them for their time and consideration.

To write a solid hero story, follow this formula:

Introduction + **Obstacle in your way** + **How you overcame it** = *What you learned*

For example, you may be from a different country and had to learn not only a new language but also a new culture. This experience taught you adaptability, determination, and creative thinking as you navigated new waters. Another example might be that you worked with a start-up and had to help the founder build the company from the ground up and now, thanks to your organizational skills and business savvy, the company is thriving. This should not be a long story, but it should highlight a key part of what you can bring to the table.

→ Now that you know the basics of writing a cover letter, use this space to help make your own. Jot down ideas for your own hero story or for things you want to highlight when you write your own cover letter.

STEP 3: THE INTERVIEW

So you've created an amazing resume and cover letter that got the hiring manager's attention. Now it's time for the final level: the interview!

Don't panic, it's going to be fine.

While looking for a job can be stressful, getting an interview can be nerve-wracking. We are so close to what we want, and if it doesn't go perfectly, we'll end up back at square one—especially if we have to go through multiple rounds of interviews for one job. Fortunately, here are some tips and tricks on how to make this process go a little smoother and help get you that job. Even if this isn't your first rodeo, it doesn't hurt to get a refresher on some interview dos and don'ts.

DO

BE PREPARED Make sure you have researched the company to know what they are about; be certain you know what job you are applying for, and even look into which department you'd be working in. Arming yourself with knowledge can help you feel confident with your interview answers and even help you ask good questions, not to mention impress your interviewer by knowing so much about the company and your field.

TALK ABOUT YOUR ACHIEVEMENTS It's always important to bring up things you achieved, as it can help your interviewer see your best qualities and how you can become a successful part of the team. Don't be afraid to talk yourself up whenever the opportunity arises. It's not bragging, and interviewers expect this.

ASK QUESTIONS You are expected to ask questions during the job interview. After all, you are going to be spending a lot of your waking hours there; you should know what you're getting into. Remember, it's not just whether they want you to work for them, it's also about whether you want to work for them. (If you're at a loss for what to ask, turn the page for some ideas.)

ASK ABOUT THE NEXT STEPS Asking about what happens after this interview can help you prepare while also showing your interest in the position.

DON'T:

STALK YOUR HIRING MANAGER ONLINE In the age of social media, it's easy to find people online, including the people interviewing you. However, do not try to follow or friend request your interviewer on social media before the interview or mention things you found online about them during the interview—it's weird.

LIE ABOUT YOUR ABILITIES While it's common to "pad" your resume a bit, it's not great to lie about critical skills that are important to the job. Don't outwardly lie about your skills and experience, especially something that can be checked. Don't be surprised if they call a company you name on your resume or make you do a coding test to see if you actually have the skill. Lying can easily burn bridges.

OUTWARDLY ASK ABOUT MONEY One of the oldest interview taboos is to ask about how much money you'll be getting paid. While this is an old taboo, many hiring managers can get annoyed if you directly ask about salary, especially if that's your first and only question. If the job posting lists the salary, ask about the types of benefits or opportunities for growth (stipends for classes, onsite childcare, etc.). If the salary isn't listed, ask about it during the end of the interview in a tactful way: "What is your budget for this position?" "How are employees compensated for this position?" You don't want to go through all of this for a job that pays lower than what you expected.

ASK IF YOU GOT THE JOB Most companies see a lot of candidates; assuming you are the only one or that your interview was so good will make you seem arrogant. Stay humble!

Here are some end-of-interview questions to ask:

What do the day-to-day responsibilities look like in this role?

How is success measured in this role?

Is there anything in my resume you were curious about?

What was your best day on the job?

Why was this position open?

What would you say the culture is like at this company?

What are the prospects for growth and advancement?

Do you provide professional development opportunities?

SO YOU GOT THE JOB: NOW WHAT?

You did it! Now the hard part begins: actually doing the job you were hired for. Whether this is your first adult job or your hundredth, here are some pointers to help make you be the adult they hired.

SET BOUNDARIES While we all love to watch a good workplace comedy, remember that life isn't a sitcom and, while you may be with your coworkers, bosses, and clients for a good chunk of your waking hours—they are not your family. They often aren't even your friends. So set strong boundaries from day one. Obviously, different jobs may require different approaches, but here are a few of the big ones: Do not do work you are not being paid for (like answering your boss's email at 2:00 a.m. on a Saturday or doing several people's projects). Don't reveal too much personal stuff about yourself (office gossip can and will come back to haunt you). And don't make work your whole life. You can be friendly while keeping it professional.

BE ORGANIZED The biggest thing about starting a job—any job—is being organized. After the honeymoon phase, when the work starts piling up and the emails never stop, you can easily get frustrated. Find ways to stay on top of your to-do list: set timers for tasks, carve out time to tackle emails, or color-code files. Whatever works for you!

ALWAYS COMMUNICATE While strong communication skills aren't something you slap on your resume, they are essential to your working (and adulting) life. The best way to survive and thrive in your career is through clear and open communication. If you can't work a certain day or do not have the bandwidth to do a specific task, let people know. Don't just say yes and figure it out later—it will go poorly. On the same note, if you want more responsibility or projects, or just want to network with others in your career, be open about that. People often appreciate the honesty. You don't need to play games.

According to the U.S. Census Bureau, the median family income in 1973 was $12,050 (about $83,000 in 2023 money). While 35.5 percent of those families received $15,000 or more annually, nearly 40 percent received less than $10,000—and women working full time earned $6,500, or about 57 percent of what men earned for that period. While these figures might sound low, it turns out those wages had about the same purchasing power as wages do in 2023 (adjusting for inflation), according to Pew Research. The plus side to this wage stagnation, however, is that company-sponsored benefit costs have risen nearly 23 percent since 2001. It really does pay to negotiate every dollar when you start a new job!

Starting a Business

Now that we have gone through all the steps of getting a job, you may think, "Wow, I don't want any part of that; I'm starting my own business." Starting a business from the ground up can be tough and very intimating, but it also holds many rewards, including the pride of creating something that's yours.

There are a variety of ways to have a business, from the traditional restaurants, stores, and services (plumbing, repairs, etc.) to freelance businesses including writing and photography. Thanks to technology, people can also do side hustles as businesses, including driving and shopping for others and selling handmade goods. Starting a business can bring many opportunities and challenges, so let's see if it's the right path for you!

BUSINESS CHECKLIST

Check all that applies. Remember, this list isn't to talk you into or out of starting a business, it's just to help you think about the skills and tools you may need to begin your journey.

○ I have a unique skill or passion that sets me apart.	○ I have the training and tools that can help me start my business (degrees, licenses, special equipment, etc.)
○ I understand the business and tax laws in my area and can follow them.	○ I am organized and can easily stick to a schedule.
○ I have money saved to help me through the starter period of my business.	○ I know exactly how many people to hire and how I can pay them.
○ I am able to take on multiple roles when needed (bookkeeping, management, creative, etc.).	○ I have strong leadership abilities and can make hard decisions.

○ I am self-motivated and driven.

○ I am confident in my ability to market myself and spread the word about my business.

○ I have reasonable expectations and know when things are and aren't possible.

○ I strive to satisfy people, but I am not a people pleaser.

○ I am able to acknowledge my mistakes and set things right.

○ I know when to ask for help and pay people for the things I cannot do (lawyers, accountants, social media managers, etc.).

○ I am able to stick to a budget.

○ I know my market and have a business plan.

○ I can do all the paperwork needed to set my business up for success (licenses, permits, insurance, logos, copyright, etc.).

○ I have a strong vision of what I want my business to eventually be.

○ I am not afraid of failure.

○ I have faith in my abilities.

Career Goals

→ Now that we have a better understanding of how to be an employed adult, it's time for you to create some goals to climb the ladder of success (if you want). Write down a list of some of your big career goals.

→ Now, take one goal and break it down into smaller actions that can help you achieve it. For example, if your goal is to have your own business, some of your actionable tasks may be to do some market research, create a website, practice your skill, etc. Choose at least three smaller actions and write them here.

→ What is your motivation for achieving this goal? Why do you want to? What does it mean for your maturity and growth?

→ Imagine, for a moment, that you have reached that goal. Picture how good it feels. Write about it as a promise to yourself. Also come up with smaller rewards for the smaller tasks you've created. For example, if you apply to three jobs this week, you'll treat yourself to a movie night—with popcorn.

Your major reward:

Mini rewards:

HEALTHY HABITS TRACKER

Goal	Mon	Tue	Wed
	◯	◯	◯
	◯	◯	◯
	◯	◯	◯
	◯	◯	◯
	◯	◯	◯
	◯	◯	◯
	◯	◯	◯
	◯	◯	◯
	◯	◯	◯
	◯	◯	◯
	◯	◯	◯
	◯	◯	◯
	◯	◯	◯
	◯	◯	◯

Rewards for the week:

Motivation:

WEEK OF

Thu	Fri	Sat	Sun	
○	○	○	○	
○	○	○	○	
○	○	○	○	
○	○	○	○	
○	○	○	○	
○	○	○	○	
○	○	○	○	
○	○	○	○	
○	○	○	○	
○	○	○	○	
○	○	○	○	
○	○	○	○	
○	○	○	○	
○	○	○	○	

What to improve for next week:

You are on your way to being your most meaningfully employed adult self. However, you don't have to do this alone. Use the habit tracker on the previous page to keep track of your goals and turn mindful actions into healthy adulting habits. And don't forget to reward yourself and claim your badges on the next page.

→ **How adult do you feel right now?**

(1)—(2)—(3)—(4)—(5)—(6)—(7)—(8)—(9)—(10)

still getting the hang of it ⟵⟶ best grown-up around

→ **Final thoughts:**

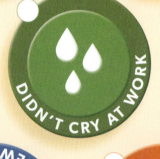

CHAPTER 5

HOME IS WHERE THE ADULT IS

(That's You)

When we were young, most of us thought about the home we would have when we were grown up. A space that was completely ours where we could do whatever we wanted, whenever we wanted. After all: our house, our rules, right? From dreaming about how to decorate, to the neighborhoods we would live in to raise our own families, it all just seemed so magical.

However, as we got older, the glamour of homeownership started to dim. No one tells you when you're putting together vision boards of dream homes that chairs are so expensive and that the water heater can break. "Homeowner" has also become more difficult in today's world thanks to a variety of factors including economic reasons and the housing crisis; so much so that many adults are choosing to rent (at unfortunately sky-high prices) or even to live with family to keep costs down. While homeownership has changed dramatically, the idea of *home* hasn't. Every person should have a place to live, a place where they can feel safe and loved. A place of their own.

Whether you are looking to rent an apartment in the big city, buy a house of your own, or live in a multi-generational household, we'll navigate the ups and downs of securing a home to help you find your place in this world.

Before we get started, let's do a brief check-in:

→ How at home do you feel right now? Explain why you feel this way.

1 — 2 — 3 — 4 — 5 — 6 — 7 — 8 — 9 — 10

can I crash here tonight? ← → there's no place like home

→ What is your current housing situation like? Write about how you got here and what you like and dislike about it.

→ What does your "dream home" look like? Don't be afraid to go into details, including the location and who may live with you.

→ Home is meant to be a safe place. What does safety mean to you?

→ What do you think your challenges will be when getting the home of your dreams, either in obtaining it or after it's been acquired?

→ What was your favorite place to live in? Your childhood home? Your first apartment after college? The house with the little garden out back? What was it about that place that was so special to you? How do you want to recreate it in your life now?

The Language of Home Buying

Getting into the realm of home ownership, even just thinking about it, can be very intimating. How do you even start? Fortunately, knowing the language of home buying can help you build confidence and prevent you from getting stuck in a crappy situation. Here are just a few general terms you should have in your adulting vocabulary.

APPRAISAL The estimated value of a house and its land made by an independent licensed professional. The appraisal is a primary factor when determining the mortgage.

ARM MORTGAGE An adjustable-rate mortgage is a mortgage with a lower interest rate at the start, which grows over time, though usually with a preset limit.

CLOSING The last stage of the home-buying process where everything has been done and the sale has been finalized.

DEBT-TO-INCOME RATIO (DTI) A measurement that a bank or loaning firm uses to estimate how to pay things back, like a mortgage or loan. It calculates the amount of income the buyer has versus the amount of debt that is held. Ideally, your DTI should be at 35 percent or less to qualify for a home loan.

DOWN PAYMENT The amount you pay at closing when you are buying a home. This isn't the full amount of the cost of the house; it's the amount of money you pay up front to make what you owe overall—and your monthly mortgage payments—less. Some loans allow for lower down payments.

ESCROW A financial agreement where money is held by a third party on behalf of two other parties while they are in the process of completing a transaction. Usually, it's to hold the buyer's money while closing the house.

EQUITY The difference between how much your home is worth and how much you owe on your mortgage.

FHA LOAN A Federal Housing Administration Loan is a home mortgage that is insured by the government and issued by a bank or lender. It is made for buyers with lower income and credit scores. While this loan is a little more lenient, it requires up-front and annual premium mortgage insurance.

FIXED-RATE MORTGAGE Also known as an FRT, this is a mortgage with a set interest rate that does not change, usually lasting around 30 years.

MORTGAGE A loan to help purchase a home or land. Buyers make payments on the loan until it is paid off, then the buyer legally owns the home. If they do not pay, the bank or lender can take the property (called a foreclosure).

PRE-APPROVAL A written agreement from a lender pre-approving a buyer for a loan of a certain amount of money. This helps buyers when shopping for a home, providing proof that they have money or can get money to purchase the property. Note: You can often be pre-approved for more money than you're comfortable spending every month on a mortgage payment, so it's important to know what that monthly payment will be before looking for homes in a certain price range.

PRE-QUALIFICATION A less official version of being pre-approved where the document says a potential loan is at a certain amount, though; the lender isn't obligated to follow through.

To Own or To Rent

Buying a home has always been a part of the "American dream"; however, homeownership often comes with a lot of responsibilities and challenges, and it's not always realistic, especially when living in a city. There are a lot of benefits to renting apartments and houses that many people might not be aware of. To help you decide which is better for you, here's a handy guide.

OWNING

- Helps build equity and credit
- Able to decorate and add whatever you want to it, have pets, etc.
- Responsible for your own repairs and maintenance
- Can make or lose money when housing prices rise and fall
- Provides a sense of stability
- Hassle to move
- Property taxes and homeowner's insurance (both of which almost always increase)
- Is an investment

RENTING

- Rent is often the same throughout the duration of the lease (though it can increase)
- May not be allowed to decorate how you want (painting the walls, adding a garden, etc.) or have pets
- Landlords handle repairs and maintenance
- Landlords can often raise rent or sell the property after the lease is up
- Can do rent-to-own (renting with the option to buy when the lease is up)
- Can move easily when lease ends
- Do not have to pay property taxes (but should choose renter's insurance)
- Is not an investment

HOME REFLECTION QUESTIONS

→ Do you prefer to rent or own at this point of your life, and why?

→ What are some obstacles to renting or buying? What are some things you can do to overcome them?

→ Do you see your preference changing at some point? What is your ultimate goal for having a home: Renting? Buying? Having a second home (e.g., woodsy cabin, beach cottage, ski condo, pied-à-terre)?

Upkeep and Maintenance

*Okay, so you did it. You got a place to live, yay! *clapping* However, having a place of your own isn't so easy. When you're on your own, you have to do a lot of upkeep and maintenance to make sure your home looks nice (and is safe to live in) and to prevent any problems down the line. We all know how to do basic things like cleaning the dishes and washing the floors, but how often should you do it? Since it's possible that no one ever explained this to you, here is a list of general upkeep and timelines to help you keep your house in order. Remember, this is just a suggested list, as your own home needs will vary (and we're not here to judge you!).*

HOUSEHOLD CHORES

DAILY TASKS
Make beds
Load or empty dishwasher/do dishes
Wipe down counters, tables, and sinks
Put things in their proper place

WEEKLY TASKS
Dust hard surfaces
Vacuum and mop
Wipe and disinfect countertops (Note: never mix bleach and ammonia)
Clean mirrors
Scrub and disinfect kitchen and bathroom sinks
Scrub toilet(s)
Scrub shower and tub
Do laundry (Note: clean the dryer's lint trap before each use)
Toss food that's expired

MONTHLY TASKS

Scrub stovetop and burner grates

Wipe down kitchen cabinets

Clean and deodorize the microwave

Vacuum couch(es) and other upholstery

Dust ceiling fan(s) and vents

EVERY 6 MONTHS

Vacuum mattress(es)	Clean blinds and curtains
Dust lampshade(s)	Shake out rugs
Scrub grout	Wash windows
Clean refrigerator and freezer	Clean and descale coffee maker

EVERY 12 MONTHS

Pull out larger appliances and furniture to clean behind and underneath

Wipe down walls

Clean dryer duct

Empty and clean cabinet shelves

Clean out/organize closets, junk drawers, medicine cabinets

ADULTING HACK

If cleaning feels like an overwhelming task, choose just one room a day to work on. For example, Monday can be the kitchen, Tuesday living room, Wednesday bathroom, Thursday entryway, Friday bedrooms, Saturday laundry, and Sunday rest.

HOME MAINTENANCE

MONTHLY TASKS	
Pay all bills	Replenish the first aid kit
Clean garbage disposal	Clear your pipes so they don't clog
Deep clean dishwasher	Check HVAC filters
Check water softener and heater	Inspect and clean vents
Test carbon monoxide detectors, smoke detectors, and fire extinguisher	

EVERY SPRING	
Repair and/or replace screens and windows	Clean screens and outdoor furniture
Lawn care (remove weeds, leaves, and debris)	Prune trees
Check your exterior siding	Re-caulk bathtub, shower, and sink
Hire professional chimney cleaner and get a safety check	Mulch flower beds
Tune lawnmower	Repair driveway and sidewalk
Inspect and repair fencing or retaining walls	Power wash front of house
Have HVAC system serviced/inspect A/C window units	

EVERY SUMMER	
Clean garage	Seal exterior cracks in windows and doors
Check deck for any damages	Inspect and repair sprinklers
Pest control	Clean and open pool
Mow lawn and perform other lawn care tasks weekly	

EVERY FALL	
Test heating system to make sure it's working	Have roof inspected and cleaned
Clear and inspect rain gutters	Have HVAC or boiler serviced
Rake leaves	Shut off exterior sprinklers and valves
Close pool	Clean dryer vent

EVERY WINTER	
Inspect basement and/or attic for pests and leaks	Vacuum refrigerator coils
Insulate exterior pipes to prevent freezing	Upgrade winter storm essentials: shovels, snowplow, generator, flashlights, ice melt, etc.
Check for icicles and ice dams in gutters	Inspect and tighten hardware

ADULTING HACK: SET UP YOUR BILLS FOR AUTOPAY

Even if you've learned how to write a check *and* mail it in on time, why bother when automatic online payments are so easy? You can pay mortgage and property taxes, as well as electric and heating bills, Wi-Fi, and other recurring bills, setting them to be withdrawn from your bank account on a certain day every month. You can often pay additional unexpected home maintenance bills (gutter cleaning, fixing a broken window, getting a pool, etc.) online as well. Check if there are additional fees for online payments (though they're probably not much more than the cost of a stamp).

HOUSEHOLD REFLECTION QUESTIONS

→ What are your favorite household tasks? What do you like about doing them?

→ What are your least favorite household tasks? Why do you find them such a challenge?

→ Brainstorm some ways you can make your least favorite household tasks easier/more bearable.

ADULTING CHALLENGE

Using the habit tracker on page 154, pick something from the previous lists and do it every day for a week. It can be the same task every day, like making your bed, or you can do a different task every day, especially ones you've been avoiding like cleaning the gutters or scrubbing grout. When you succeed, claim your badge on page 157.

How to Make a House a Home

Okay, so we covered how to take care of your house, but how do you make it a home? Home should be a safe place where you can find comfort and shelter from the cold and scary outside world. Whether you're moving into your first home with a mortgage or you're living on your own for the first time, here are some tips on how to make a house a home. You don't have to be a professional DIY-er to do all these tasks. Do what you're comfortable with, and don't be afraid to ask for help.

DECORATE YOUR SPACE WITH PERSONAL TOUCHES Adding family photos, art pieces, trinkets, etc. can really help a place feel like yours.

INVEST IN YOUR BED You'll be spending a lot of time there, so splurge on a comfortable mattress, a good headboard, nice sheets, and a comforter you love.

ADD YOUR FAVORITE COLORS No surprise here, but adding your favorite colors makes you happy. If you can't paint your walls, add a splash of color with your furniture, curtains, appliances, etc.

USE ALL OF YOUR SENSES It's not just about how your home looks, it's about what it smells like and how it feels, as well. Add softness with fluffy blankets or overstuffed armchairs. Light candles or add flowers for a lovely scent. You can also use your Bluetooth speaker to play soft music when you're relaxing at home.

MAKE SPACE FOR WHAT YOU LOVE A house or apartment isn't just where you keep all your stuff or where you go to sleep every night; it should be a place you interact with often and look forward to doing things in. One way to do that is by making space for your favorite hobbies and activities. Even in a small space, you can carve out a corner to do your painting or other art projects. If you like to garden, create a space inside and out for it. Same with exercising, cooking, meditation, and music making. Whether you have a big house or a small apartment, make it a place to do what makes you happy.

CREATE MEMORIES The best way to make a house a home is to create lasting memories there. From hosting parties and cookouts with your friends and neighbors, to raising a family, creating special moments to treasure can make a place feel special. They don't have to be big moments. Cuddling with your puppy on a snowy night, making cookies with your partner, and savoring quiet morning coffees can often leave a more lasting impression than big moments.

ADULTING CHALLENGE

Choose something from these pages to make your space your home. It can be something big or small, but make a conscious effort to make it your own. When you succeed, claim your badge on page 157.

Home Goals

→ Now that we have a better understanding of how to be an amazing home-bound adult, it's time to come up with some goals to create your dream home. Write down a list of some of your big home goals.

→ Now, take one goal and break it down into smaller actions that can help you achieve it. For example, if your goal is to buy a house, some of your actionable tasks may be to do some research on homes in your area, meet with a loan offer, and create a budget. Choose at least three smaller actions and write them here.

→ What is your motivation for achieving this goal? Why do you want to? What does it mean for your maturity and growth?

→ Imagine, for a moment, that you have reached that goal. Picture how good it feels. Write about it as a promise to yourself. Also come up with smaller rewards for the smaller tasks you've created. For example, if you did some home repairs this week, treat yourself to a dinner out.

Your major reward:

Mini rewards:

HEALTHY HABITS TRACKER

Goal	Mon	Tue	Wed
	○	○	○
	○	○	○
	○	○	○
	○	○	○
	○	○	○
	○	○	○
	○	○	○
	○	○	○
	○	○	○
	○	○	○
	○	○	○
	○	○	○
	○	○	○
	○	○	○

Rewards for the week:

Motivation:

WEEK OF

Thu	Fri	Sat	Sun	
○	○	○	○	
○	○	○	○	
○	○	○	○	
○	○	○	○	
○	○	○	○	
○	○	○	○	
○	○	○	○	
○	○	○	○	
○	○	○	○	
○	○	○	○	
○	○	○	○	
○	○	○	○	
○	○	○	○	
○	○	○	○	

What to improve for next week:

You are on your way to having an adult roof over your head. However, you don't have to do this alone. Use the habit tracker on the previous page to keep track of your goals and turn mindful actions into healthy adulting habits. And don't forget to reward yourself and claim your badges on the next page.

→ How adult do you feel right now?

(1)—(2)—(3)—(4)—(5)—(6)—(7)—(8)—(9)—(10)

still getting the hang of it ← ——————→ best grown-up around

→ Final thoughts:

CHAPTER 6

YOU AND ME

How to Have Healthy Relationships

One of the most difficult tasks of becoming an adult isn't buying a home or paying bills; it's trying to make friends with other adults. It seems like during our mid-twenties and early thirties there are fewer and fewer opportunities to make friends, especially after certain life changes like making a major move, getting married, or having children. While technology has made it easier to stay connected to friends we make during different stages of our lives, and helps us make new friends all over the globe, it's also very isolating. It can be difficult to see people on social media having the time of their lives while you're hanging out at home alone. Or seeing your friends from high school getting married and having kids while you get ghosted on a dating app.

While social media doesn't portray an accurate version of real life, it does highlight how secluded our worlds can be. We are often cut off from our community, don't know our neighbors, and have very few opportunities to meet other adults unless they are online. While we may seem lonelier than ever, we don't have to be. In this chapter, we'll talk about how to build and strengthen relationships of all kinds and how to be alone without feeling lonely.

Before we get started, let's do a brief check-in:

→ How social do you feel right now?

$1 - 2 - 3 - 4 - 5 - 6 - 7 - 8 - 9 - 10$

sole member of the ←   → my social life has
lonely-hearts club   never been better

→ Explain why you feel this way.

_____

_____

_____

_____

_____

_____

_____

_____

_____

→ What does your social life currently look like? Who are the people you see the most?

→ What does your love life look like?

→ When was your last big heartbreak? This can be a romantic relationship ending, a friend breakup, or a dramatic falling out with a coworker. Write about what happened and what, if anything, you learned from it.

→ Who is the person you have the strongest relationship with right now? Why are they your person?

→ Do you feel lonely? In what ways do you feel lonely, and in what ways do you want to connect with others?

→ Write about your ideal relationships. This can be a romantic relationship, your social life, your relationship with your family, or all of the above.

How to Meet New People as an Adult

Oh, to be young again, where your best friend was the person who went to the same school as you or someone you got assigned to room with in college. Sadly, when we get a little older and more established and stable in our lives, that's usually around the time we stop making friends. It's not that we become less lovable, friendly, or exciting, it's just that our routine of getting up, going to work, running errands, and going to sleep leaves little time for socializing with new people (doubly so if you add kids to the mix). Not to mention our society typically values romantic relationships more than platonic ones, meaning that we spend most of our social time looking for romantic love rather than friendship, which can often lead to isolation as we put all of our social needs on one person.

Whether you have a romantic partner or not, it's important to have friends as an adult, people to share your ups and downs and act as your support system through the messiness of life. If you're at a loss, here are some ways adults can make friends. (Bonus: These tips also work if you are looking for a love interest.)

FIND A LOCAL HOBBY GROUP It doesn't matter if you met your fifth-grade best friend at band camp or you always hung out with your rugby teammates in college; you became friends because you both shared the same interest. Well, the same principle applies to making friends as an adult. Look around your community for groups, clubs, and teams you may be interested in like:

- a local softball league
- a women's hiking club
- a pug enthusiasts' group
- a beachcomber's club
- a Revolutionary War reenactment group
- a game night collective at a local coffeeshop.

TAKE A CLASS If meeting people through classes still feels most comfortable, go ahead and sign up for things like art, yoga, Italian for beginners, knitting, cake decorating, archery, aikido, landscaping with perennials, infant swim—if you can think it, there's a class for it. Area colleges, community centers, craft stores, libraries, and bookstores offer all manner of classes, many for a nominal fee.

VOLUNTEER People who volunteer their time often do so for something they're passionate about, so what better way to find like-minded people to befriend? Try:

- animal shelters, where you can often walk, brush, or read to animals awaiting adoption
- food banks
- Habitat for Humanity
- the Red Cross
- being a docent at a children's or historical museum
- volunteering translation services
- reading to the blind
- helping clean up trails for the National Park Service (or your local nature preserve or park).

TRY ONLINE Online isn't just for dating! More and more apps are catering to people who are looking to be "just friends" (for reals). This is a great way to make new friends, as it clearly shows that both parties are looking for friendship, so you don't have to feel awkward. If you're not comfortable with apps, scroll your social media feed for groups that people you already know are part of, or search for groups meeting up in your area.

MAKE THE FIRST MOVE While meeting new people can be nerve-wracking, sometimes to make lasting friendships, you're going to have to make the first move—whether it's cocktail hour at a friend's wedding, a parent group, or just your neighbor. You don't need to say, "Please be my friend!" but start by making small talk. "I love your outfit!" or "I just moved to town. What do you recommend for takeout?" or even "Your dog is so cute. Can I pet him?" Break the ice by being nice.

STEP OUTSIDE YOUR COMFORT ZONE The definition of insanity is doing the same thing over again and expecting different results, so if you're asking why you haven't made new friends or found "the one" already, you may want to start by looking at your routines. If you keep doing the same things (driving to work, not talking to anyone at work, running errands, going home, staying home), it's going to be hard to meet new people. Break out of your comfort zone and say yes to things. Accept that invite to your cousin's party, go to the neighborhood potluck, shake things up!

STAY POSITIVE Feeling alone as an adult can really be depressing, but don't let your fear and sorrow cut you off from meeting new people. Believe that you will meet the people who will love and support you, and the rest should fall into place.

ADULTING CHALLENGE

Try making a new friend during the upcoming month using one or more of these suggestions. You can even add "putting yourself out there" to your habit tracker on page 176 if you wish. When completed, claim your badge on page 179.

The Care and Maintenance of Relationships

They don't teach you how to be a good friend or partner in school. Once you've made connections and feel you have tentative friendships, it's often hard to maintain and care for those relationships, especially when our own lives get so busy and stressful that we may forget about taking care of others. If you struggle with wanting to be there for others but you're not sure where to begin, take a look at this checklist to see what you're doing right and get suggestions on what you could be doing differently. (Note: this checklist works for all relationships!)

○ Make plans and stick to them.

○ Ask them about their day.

○ Show yourself kindness. (Remember, by developing a healthy relationship with yourself, you can create good relationships with others. Think of it as practicing kindness with yourself.)

○ Allow yourself to be vulnerable with another person (for example, talk about a bad day, don't lie when something is wrong, feel like you are your true self, etc.).

○ Hold space for others (for example, let people open up to you without judging them, listen while they vent, hold them while they cry, etc.).

○ Do something kind for no reason (bring them coffee, buy their favorite candy, give them flowers, etc.).

○ Remember birthdays.

○ Support them through wins and losses.

○ Engage in healthy conversation when there's a disagreement instead of doing anything to get your way.	○ Listen when people say you hurt them, and make efforts to change.
○ Send texts to check in.	○ Tell people when they have hurt you.
○ Actively listen.	○ Support and respect another's dreams and interests.
○ Respect boundaries.	○ Have realistic expectations for people.
○ Affirm the feelings of others.	○ Be honest without being mean.
○ Don't make people read your mind.	○ Come into every relationship in good faith.

ADULTING CHALLENGE

For one week, do one or more of the suggestions in the checklist. It can be as simple as texting a friend about their day or being honest with your sibling about something that bothers you. Keep track of it using your habit tracker on page 176. When completed, claim your badge on page 179.

How to End a Relationship

A sad fact about adulthood is learning that not all relationships are made to last. Some relationships gradually fade or shift to something different. Some relationships end peacefully with a loving goodbye. And some relationships end bitterly with many fights and tears. What do you do when you care about someone, but your lives are moving in different directions? When you've outgrown a relationship with someone you've spent years with? Or even when moving out of a home you once shared with someone?

Ending a relationship is difficult, especially if you have no hard feelings toward the other person. While it may be tempting to ghost the other person or even force them to end things with you so you can avoid responsibility, the adult thing to do is to end the relationship by being direct and honest so that you can both move on. If nothing else, think about running into them at a wedding in a year, or bumping into a mutual friend at the market next week: do you want it to be awkward or cordial? Here are some tips on how to end a relationship, the adult way.

KNOW WHEN IT'S TIME TO LEAVE Often, it's easy to stay in a relationship simply because it's easier, even if it isn't as good as it once was, than to leave and have to meet new people and build new relationships. However, it's not healthy to stay in a dead-end relationship and wait for the end to become bitter. Once you realize there is no way to save the relationship (even if you've tried everything), it's time to let it go. Trust us, it's much kinder for them (and you) in the long run.

SCHEDULE IT This may sound a little cold at first, but scheduling a breakup will make it more likely that you will end it and do so in a more controlled, thoughtful way. It's tempting to brush it off, thinking, "I'll do it next week," but then next week their dog has to go the vet, and you don't want to pile on, so you keep pushing it off until eventually you get into a major fight and everything comes out. If you want to end things on a clean note, schedule a time and place to do it, like inviting them over for coffee or going out to dinner. Give them a heads up about what this is about so they don't go in blind.

BE HONEST ABOUT YOUR FEELINGS When you do start the breakup, be direct about your feelings, how things got to this point, and why you want to go separate ways. You don't have to be callous ("I don't want to be friends with you because you're boring now."), but you shouldn't lie to save their feelings ("It's not you, it's me."). By being honest about your feelings, you're letting the other person have closure and develop an understanding instead of being blindsided or feeling bad about themselves.

LISTEN Obviously, they are going to have something to say about this; after all, they were a member of this relationship. It's important to listen to what the other person has to say and answer any questions they may have. Maybe they are feeling the same way. Maybe they want to know if they did something wrong. Be kind, go over any questions they may have, and talk it through with them. A breakup is just like any other conversation, just with a more permanent ending.

TALK ABOUT THE NEXT STEPS One thing about relationships as an adult is learning that not all breakups have to lead to a lot of drama and burned bridges. While some breakups do lead to staying out of each other's lives and eventually blocking numbers, it doesn't have to be like that. If you still want to be in this person's life but not as close, talk about that. Talk about needing space or wanting to set up new boundaries in your dynamic. Talk about how the ending of the relationship looks for you, especially if you share children, animals, or property. While creating a new dynamic can take time and healing, it doesn't have to be a no-contact situation.

RELATIONSHIP REFLECTION QUESTIONS

→ How do you feel you can best show up for the people in your life?

→ How do you feel you can improve a current relationship?

→ Think of one of your relationships, either a romantic partnership or a friendship you cherish. Do you feel like there's an equal balance of give and take in your relationship? Who is doing most of the giving and taking?

Coping with Loneliness

The adult world can be a pretty lonely place sometimes. Even when you're surrounded by loved ones, you can still feel alone. When we feel lonely, we may do some unhealthy things, including people pleasing, clinging to toxic relationships, drowning in unhappy feelings, turning to harmful self-soothing practices like overeating or drinking, and other unhealthy coping methods that can make our lives and our feelings of loneliness worse.

We're conditioned from a young age to want to be included in things, from that kindergarten birthday party to the senior prom. Though we've outgrown our school ties, social media can lure even the adultest of adults back in, creating FOMO, or fear of missing out, where we become preoccupied with the thought that others are having a fun experience without us. But being alone doesn't mean you have to be lonely. When you learn to enjoy your own company, you'll find that your quality of life and your self-esteem get a major lift. Here are some healthy ways to cope with loneliness and become your own friend.

- Do volunteer work.
- Start a new hobby or rekindle a hobby you previously enjoyed.
- Spend time with animals.
- Take yourself on a date: dinner, museums, movies, vacations, etc.

ADULTING CHALLENGE

If you've been feeling lonely, try to get out of the habit of loneliness by doing one (or more) of these activities for one week. Add it to your habit tracker on page 176. When completed, claim your badge on page 179.

- Take on involved projects including: home improvement, building something, planting a flower bed, etc.
- Journal your feelings.
- Make plans for the future.
- Take a class in a subject you're interested in.
- Log off social media.
- Call a loved one.
- Try something new.
- Meditate and connect with your emotions.

If this feeling is persistent even after trying a few of these suggestions, you may want to consider talking to a therapist for extra help.

In 2023, U.S. Surgeon General Dr. Vivek H. Murthy declared loneliness a public health epidemic. In his advisory, *Our Epidemic of Loneliness and Isolation*, he wrote that half of adults experience loneliness, which can be as dangerous as smoking up to 15 cigarettes a day. Research has found that isolation can lead to sleep issues, depression and anxiety, heart disease and high blood pressure, stroke and diabetes, and dementia. To repair social connections, Dr. Murthy recommends—in addition to volunteering, sports groups, and other member organizations—utilizing other aspects of community that bring people together, such as public transportation, libraries, parks and green spaces, and playgrounds.

Relationship Goals

→ Now that we have a better understanding of how to be a sociable adult, it's time for you to come up with some goals to create your dream relationships. Write down a list of some of your big relationship goals.

→ Now, take one goal and break it down into smaller actions that can help you achieve it. For example, if your goal is to be comfortable alone, some of your actionable tasks may be to go out to dinner by yourself, create solo plans, and learn more about yourself. Choose at least three smaller actions and write them here.

→ What is your motivation for achieving this goal? Why do you want to? What does it mean for your maturity and growth?

→ Imagine, for a moment, that you have reached that goal. Picture how good it feels. Write about it as a promise to yourself. Also come up with smaller rewards for the smaller tasks you've created. For example, if you made a dating profile, treat yourself to some new shoes (for going out in!).

Your major reward:

Mini rewards:

HEALTHY HABITS TRACKER

Goal	Mon	Tue	Wed
	◯	◯	◯
	◯	◯	◯
	◯	◯	◯
	◯	◯	◯
	◯	◯	◯
	◯	◯	◯
	◯	◯	◯
	◯	◯	◯
	◯	◯	◯
	◯	◯	◯
	◯	◯	◯
	◯	◯	◯
	◯	◯	◯
	◯	◯	◯

Rewards for the week:

Motivation:

WEEK OF

Thu	Fri	Sat	Sun	
○	○	○	○	
○	○	○	○	
○	○	○	○	
○	○	○	○	
○	○	○	○	
○	○	○	○	
○	○	○	○	
○	○	○	○	
○	○	○	○	
○	○	○	○	
○	○	○	○	
○	○	○	○	
○	○	○	○	
○	○	○	○	

What to improve for next week:

You are on your way to having true adult relationships. However, you don't have to do this alone. Use the habit tracker on the previous page to keep track of your goals and turn mindful actions into healthy adulting habits. And don't forget to reward yourself and claim your badges on the next page.

→ How adult do you feel right now?

1 — 2 — 3 — 4 — 5 — 6 — 7 — 8 — 9 — 10

still getting the hang of it ←——————→ best grown-up around

→ Final thoughts:

Your Next Steps:

Going Out into the Adult World

You did it! You made it to the end of the book. Congratulations! *throws confetti* While our journey together may be over, this is only the first step in your adulting adventure. We hope this book helps give you the tools to help build the life you deserve to live. Remember, this is only the first step; the rest of the journey is yours to take.

Because we are so proud of you, here is your final badge:

Welcome to the adult world! You're going to do amazing things!

Now that we've come to the end of the book, take a moment to reflect on your journey.

→ How adult do you feel right now?

① — ② — ③ — ④ — ⑤ — ⑥ — ⑦ — ⑧ — ⑨ — ⑩

still getting the hang of it ←——————→ best grown-up around

→ Explain why you feel this way.

_____

_____

_____

_____

_____

_____

_____

→ What expectations did you have going into this book? Do you feel they were met?

_____

_____

_____

_____

_____

_____

_____

_____

_____

→ What was the hardest chapter of this book for you? Why?

→ Where did you feel you learned the most from this book? How will you use those lessons in your life?

→ What habits did you develop from this book? Do you think you will keep up with them now?

→ What is one thing that has changed in your life from the start of this book?

→ How confident do you feel in your abilities as an adult?

APPENDIX
Adulting Tips They Didn't Teach You in School

Types of Insurance You Should Have

For every phase of life, you'll have different insurance needs. (Remember, it's better to have it and not need it than to need it and not have it.) Below are some suggested guidelines, rather than a rulebook, on what insurance to have when; for example, if you own a home in your 20s, then you'll want homeowner's insurance rather than renter's.

IN YOUR 20s

HEALTH INSURANCE Health insurance is probably the most important insurance you can have. Not only can it cover physicals and specialists but also hospital visits, emergencies, medications, and surgeries; it can save you from medical debt, which can instantly wipe out your savings and put you into deep debt. While you may be healthy at this moment, you never know what the future may hold. Health insurance also provides preventive medical care (those lists in chapter 2), so you don't have to wait until there is an emergency to take care of your health. Often, health insurance is offered through your place of employment or through your spouse's employer, but you can also get insured via insurance companies themselves.

AUTO INSURANCE If you drive any vehicle, you most likely have to have auto insurance to cover any potential damages or accidents that happen on the road. Even if it's not your fault, having auto insurance can prevent major bills if anything should happen. There is a variety of car insurance—liability insurance (covers damage you cause to other cars on the road), comprehensive coverage (covers any repairs on your car if damaged and replaces your car if totaled or stolen), and collision coverage (covers the repairs on your car if you're in an accident)—though it is recommended to have all three. You can get car insurance through different private companies.

RENTER'S INSURANCE Renter's insurance protects your belongings in the apartment or home that you rent. While your landlord has insurance to protect the property, it doesn't cover anything that belongs to you, which is why it's important to have renter's insurance in case there is an accident, natural disaster, or theft. It also protects you if your home becomes unlivable because of damages. You can get renter's insurance through private companies.

DISABILITY INSURANCE If you are in the workforce, it's important to get disability insurance to protect you if something happens to you and you are unable to work, like with an accident or illness. Disability insurance gives you a percentage of your salary until you are back to work. There are two kinds of disability insurance: short-term disability (for example, you broke your leg and can't go into your construction job) and long-term disability (where it may take you years before you can work). While employers often cover short-term disability, you have to cover long-term disability on your own.

LIFE INSURANCE Bad news, everyone: you aren't going to live forever. Yes, take a minute for that to settle in. While you may not think about buying life insurance in your 20s, it's usually the best time to buy, as it's when you are usually in your best health. The longer you wait, the more it tends to cost. Life insurance is meant to protect the people you love when you pass away, giving your beneficiary a sum of money on your death. This is great if you have children or a family that'll need financial help when you pass, especially if it's sudden, or to help cover funeral costs. If you don't have dependents, you may not need it.

IN YOUR 30s

HOMEOWNER'S INSURANCE Similar to renter's insurance, homeowner's insurance protects your home and your belongings in the event of an accident or disaster. It can also protect you if an injury happens on your property, like a tree falls on your roof or a delivery person falls on your sidewalk. You can get homeowner's insurance through a private company.

PET INSURANCE Pet insurance has become very popular, as our four-legged friends can often produce some costly bills when they are not feeling well. Some plans may cover vet visits, vaccinations, and emergencies, including surgery. If you've ever had a vet bill, you'll want this insurance.

IN YOUR 40s

LONG-TERM CARE INSURANCE As we creep toward our golden years, we may find that we need more help than we used to, especially if we've been injured or ill. Long-term care insurance covers home care, assisted living, hospice, or a nursing home. This can really add up, so it's often advised to get it relatively early, so you don't have to pay for it later.

I Have to do My Own Laundry?

Yes, part of being an adult is doing your own laundry, making sure you don't shrink everything in the wash or dye your white shirts pink because you had a red sock in the mix. Here's a quick guide to understanding how to read those tags on the back of your clothes. Thank us later.

QUICK TIPS: HOW TO IRON

- Read the garment label for whether it's ok to be ironed and how hot to set the iron; for multiple items with different heat needs, start with the lowest-temp item first.
- Iron on the wrong side (inside out).
- Smooth the garment over the ironing board (or sturdy flat surface with a thick cotton towel laid over it).
- Iron clothes while slightly damp (spritz with water, use the spray or steam feature on your iron, or use spray starch).
- Use firm, slow strokes of the iron to smooth out wrinkles—and keep the iron moving!
- Do not iron over buttons, zippers, patches, embroidery, sequins, etc.
- Hang up ironed clothes immediately.

How to Apologize in 3 Easy Steps

1. **SAY YOU'RE SORRY** It's easy to try to explain your side of the story or try to make excuses so that someone won't be mad at you. However, to apologize like an adult, the first two words you need to say are, "I'm sorry."

2. **EXPLAIN WHAT HAPPENED** This is not to give excuses or shift blame like, "I'm sorry that you can't take a joke," or, "I'm sorry, but it's not my fault that traffic was terrible." Rather, it's to explain the situation. For example, "I'm sorry that I hurt you. I misunderstood what you said and I took things out of context and over-reacted, but that isn't fair to you." Or, "I'm sorry I'm late for the meeting. I know that everyone took time to come here, and I'm sorry I made people late. I simply set my alarm wrong."

3. **MAKE AMENDS AND CHANGE BEHAVIOR** Tell them what you are planning to do to make amends and how to change your behavior in the future. It can be as simple as setting a reminder on your phone so you can get to places on time, or even changing behavior like taking a time out before speaking with anger. To make an apology sincere, you need to explain how you can make this right for the future.

Note: Just because you said you're sorry doesn't mean that a person has to accept it or give you forgiveness in return. Being an adult means handling not be forgiven in a mature way. Sometimes sorry isn't enough, and you need to always respect people's feelings and boundaries.

How to Pack a Bag

No, you can't keep throwing things in your suitcase and hoping for the best. Here is how to pack a bag, the adulting way.

MAKE A LIST Make a list of everything you may need, sorting by categories: clothes, toiletry, entertainment, and important papers (passport, travelers checks, etc.). Check them off as you go.

CREATE OUTFITS BEFORE PACKING If you're traveling by plane, where every ounce counts, consider culling your essentials to just one outfit every day you are traveling, an outfit for when you come home, and a backup outfit in case something happens. Make sure that all your outfits can be mixed and matched so that a few pieces of clothing can be worn in different ways; if it all flows together, it will give you more choices.

ROLL AND FOLD Pro tip for making sure you have room in your suitcase and preventing wrinkles in your clothing: roll softer clothing and fold stiffer clothing. Items like underwear, T-shirts, jeans, and knits won't wrinkle, so roll them up and put them at the bottom of your suitcase. Fold more wrinkle-prone clothing neatly and place it on top of your rolled items. Add things like belts around the perimeter of the bag.

PLACE WHAT YOU NEED FIRST, LAST Pack the things that you'll need right away at the very top of your suitcase: a jacket, the outfit you want to wear when you arrive at your location, or anything else you may need.

BE CLEVER Packing cubes have been a blessing as they can help you pack with ease and help you find everything you need. However, you can also use items around your house to make packing easier, like putting shoes in a gallon ziptop bag (and stuffing rolled socks in the shoes) and using a pill organizer to store your jewelry.

How to Make Coffee

If you're a coffee drinker, you know how sacred this brew is to your adulting life. If you want to save money on pricy coffeeshops or expensive coffee-pops (remember Chapter 3?), here's how to make a good cup of coffee to help you get through your day of adulting. (And if you're not a coffee drinker, at some point you'll probably have a visitor who is.)

STEP 1: GATHER YOUR TOOLS

Obviously, you need the right tools and ingredients, including:

- a coffee machine (here we're using a drip coffee machine with the pot included)
- coffee filters that fit your machine (cone or basket)
- coffee grounds
- cream and sugar, if that's your thing

Later, you can get fancy with it by grinding your own coffee beans and using a French press or Moka Pot, but for your first adulting experience, let's keep it simple.

STEP 2: PREPARE YOUR COFFEE MAKER

Open the top of your coffee maker and place your filter into the filter holder. Coffee is made by having hot water drip through coffee grounds.

STEP 3: ADD YOUR COFFEE

Take a tablespoon and place 4 tablespoons of ground coffee in your filter. Four tablespoons makes about eight cups of coffee (8 ounces each), so edit your measurement as needed. Make sure the grounds are spread evenly in the filter.

STEP 4: ADD WATER

Most coffee makers will have a line on your water reservoir showing how much water is needed for how many cups; pour water up to the line of your choosing. Sometimes the water-fill line will be on your coffee pot; if so, pour the water into the water reservoir and place the coffee pot back on the burner with the handle facing you. The coffee maker will heat up your water to the right temperature.

STEP 5: TURN YOUR COFFEE POT ON AND CHECK SETTINGS

Turn on your coffee maker and check the settings; usually, it's a setting for brew strength (strong or regular). Select the kind you prefer and press the brew button.

STEP 6: BREW AND ENJOY

Wait for your coffee to brew. When completed, pour yourself a cup and enjoy this moment brought to you by your adult self!

Quarto

© 2025 Quarto Publishing Group USA Inc.

This edition published in 2025 by Chartwell Books,
an imprint of The Quarto Group
142 West 36th Street, 4th Floor
New York, NY 10018 USA
T (212) 779-4972
www.Quarto.com

Contains content originally published as *The Adulting Workbook* in 2023 by Chartwell Books.

All rights reserved. No part of this book may be reproduced in any form without written permission of the copyright owners. All images in this book have been reproduced with the knowledge and prior consent of the artists concerned, and no responsibility is accepted by producer, publisher, or printer for any infringement of copyright or otherwise, arising from the contents of this publication. Every effort has been made to ensure that credits accurately comply with information supplied. We apologize for any inaccuracies that may have occurred and will resolve inaccurate or missing information in a subsequent reprinting of the book.

10 9 8 7 6 5 4 3 2 1

Chartwell titles are also available at discount for retail, wholesale, promotional, and bulk purchase. For details, contact the Special Sales Manager by email at specialsales@quarto. com or by mail at The Quarto Group, Attn: Special Sales Manager, 100 Cummings Center Suite 265D, Beverly, MA 01915, USA.

ISBN: 978-0-7858-4647-5

Publisher: Wendy Friedman
Senior Publishing Manager: Meredith Mennitt
Designer: Kate Sinclair

All stock design elements ©Shutterstock

Printed in China

This book provides general information. It should not be relied upon as recommending or promoting any specific diagnosis or method of treatment for a particular condition. It is not intended as a substitute for medical advice or for direct diagnosis and treatment of a medical or psychological condition by a qualified physician or therapist. Readers who have questions about a particular condition, possible treatments for that condition, or possible reactions from the condition or its treatment should consult a physician, therapist, or other qualified healthcare professional. Similarly, readers who have questions about investments, home buying, or other financial matters should consult a qualified financial professional.